WHERE IS HEAVEN?

CHILDREN'S WISDOM ON FACING DEATH

BY TED MENTEN

RUNNING PRESS
PHILADELPHIA · LONDON

Canadian representatives: General Publishing Co., Ltd.,
30 Lesmill Road, Don Mills, Ontario M3B 2T6.

9   8   7   6   5   4   3   2   I
Digit on the right indicates the number of this printing.

Library of Congress Cataloging-in-Publication Number 94–67769

ISBN I–56138–525–5

Cover photograph by Barbara Peacock/FPG International Corp.
Cover design by Toby Schmidt
Interior design by Paul Kepple
Typography: Centaur MT with Schneidler Initials

This book may be ordered by mail from the publisher.
Please add $2.50 for postage and handling.
But try your bookstore first!

Running Press Book Publishers
125 South Twenty-second Street
Philadelphia, Pennsylvania 19103–4399

For my children

CONTENTS

A C K N O W L E D G M E N T S

SOME DEBTS CAN NEVER be paid, but they should be acknowledged.

I am, first of all, indebted to all the children whose lives illuminate these pages. And to their parents who, with unflinching devotion and love in the face of their ultimate despair, entrusted their children to me and, in time, came to understand the *real* work of the court jester.

To all the determined, devoted doctors and overworked, dedicated nurses who at first endured and then endorsed my foolishness, thank you. And to my good friend and mentor, Mary Williams, who singled me out, goaded me on, and remained a constant guide along this path, thank you with love.

To my friends who listen to my stories, read my manuscripts, and never complain, thank you once again. Especially Dave.

Once again, I am indebted to my editor, Dave Borgenicht, whose vision of my work is often clearer than my own, and who has done more than correct my spelling and grammar—he has helped to give this book its shape, and pushed me to do better writing when I would have rather gone to the beach.

And last, but not least, thanks to everyone at Running Press who, with their enthusiasm and support, make it easier to be an author.

PREFACE

IN MY LATE TWENTIES, like almost everyone in my generation, I found myself in therapy. I guess I was looking for answers just like everyone else, but my doctor was into assigning blame, and I wasn't, so we parted. Then I joined a group, and the only thing I learned there was that there was a talking chair, and whoever sat in that chair dominated the session.

So in Harmony, our in-hospital, nonprofessional self-therapy sessions, we have no chairs. The children and I sit in a circle on the floor or on pillows.

In Harmony we try to talk about the things that bother us in the whole process of illness and death. It is an unnatural process in an unnatural setting. Children are meant to be in school, or outdoors playing games, not confined to hospitals and hooked up to machines. But there they are in the hospitals, nonetheless, and in Harmony we try to understand the process and work out solutions to the problems that besiege them. Talking does not come easily to children in the presence of adults, but in the world of the dying there are grownups everywhere—and the grownups have all the controls.

In Harmony, I try to give kids back some control over their lives—I encourage them to talk it out themselves. The process isn't always easy or successful but we give it our best shot.

Sometimes, when the topic is a particularly difficult one, we sit with our backs against one another, and our legs form the spokes of a wheel. This is less confrontational, and we often say things openly that we might not say face-to-face.

I discovered that sitting at a table with a patient was easier than sitting in chairs facing each other. The barrier of the table offers a safe field of exchange. I often hold sessions with kids around a craft table and let them paint while we talk. Two messages emerge—one spoken, one painted. Combined, they provide a full answer.

In one-on-one conversations, I find that walking side-by-side while talking is easier than face-to-face. With children, a walk in the park, or at the beach is wonderful for opening up. With adults, driving in a car works just as well.

I love offering hugs to kids, but many times they don't want that. It violates their space. Confrontation is a big problem for children who have been ill for a long time. They feel terribly vulnerable, and are shy with strangers, unsure if this new person has a big needle behind his back. But often, the same child that refused to be hugged will not refuse a piggyback ride, and will shout in your ear to bounce harder, and run faster.

As time passed, I learned to let the children lead me in the direction they needed to go.

I seldom introduce a topic in Harmony. Rather, I let the children bring up the subjects they have on their minds at the moment.

Or, if I know that they have a particular topic in mind (say, the recent death of one member of the group), I quiz the most open member of the group, and let it flow from there. For the most part, the less I say the better. Self-healing is the strongest medicine, and it is best prescribed by one another.

This book is about children who face death every day of their lives. About how the innocent beauty of their hearts and minds can guide us along the path to eventual understanding and acceptance—of the mystery of death and the miracle of life.

What follows is a compilation of conversations from the Harmony groups. These are from notes and tapes, and have been edited for clarity. I hope that I have not lost the children's voices, and that in their conversations we will hear the truth of their feelings about life and death and the process of dying.

And perhaps we will come away with some truths of our own.

INTRODUCTION

LIKE MILLIONS OF OTHER healthy people, I have a natural aversion to hospitals. The pale green walls, the dim lighting, the pervasive fragrance of antiseptic, and the superstition that this was "the place that people come to die," all combined to make me less than enthusiastic about joining my friends on a beautiful sunny Sunday to bring teddy bears to children at a local hospital.

"You'll get a feather if you go," stated my friend Helen.

"They give you a feather?" I replied, puzzled by the idea.

"No, they don't, but God will. Every time you do a good thing, God gives you a feather . . . for your wings in heaven."

Considering the depth of my self-indulgence over the almost fifty years of my life, one feather seemed like a drop in the proverbial bucket. But they say that every journey begins with a single step. That bright Sunday morning was the first step on a journey that changed my life forever.

When you are named Ted, every clever person knows what to give you as a gift on special occasions—a teddy bear. From my first days in the crib, I was surrounded by them. On every birthday and holiday, I received more bears. Over the years, hundreds of them filled shelves and sat in chairs all around me.

I suppose I should have outgrown them, but I didn't. Once, when I was fifteen, I decided that having a roomful of teddy bears was unmanly, and I put them up in the attic. That night I had terrible nightmares about them dying in the attic from lack of affection, and I brought them all back downstairs and pledged my undying devotion to them all. Manly or not, these guys had seen me through thick and thin, and I was honor-bound to love them. Their ever-constant smiles and watchful eyes had protected and delighted me from day-to-day. They still do.

So, on that fateful Sunday morning, armed with a knapsack full of brand-new teddy bears, I joined my friends in front of the hospital.

When we had all assembled, Helen guided us through the maze of halls until we reached the children's ward. We were greeted by dozens of smiling faces as we entered the room.

"Say 'good morning' children," ordered their starched nurse.

"Good morning," chimed the children.

That ended the formalities, and the free-for-all began. Within moments they were out of their beds and dancing around us as we handed out the teddy bears. Screams of delight filled the air as the furry critters found new life in the arms of their new friends. Names were given, histories were created, and a good time was had by all. The last thing I remember from that first day was the sight of dozens of kids, curled up asleep with a new teddy in their arms. At that perfect moment I didn't care about the feather—this was my reward.

In the months that followed, I went back every Sunday, sometimes with my friends, but more often than not by myself. I was like a junkie who needed a fix—a fix on life. In those hours with the children, I found a calm and a joy that I had not found anywhere else. *I* thought that I was comforting them, but I found that *they* were comforting me. And through them I found my own inner innocence and joy. The innocence and joy of simply being alive.

P R O L O G U E

I WAS DREAMING. Above my head the moon danced through the barren branches of the trees. I remember thinking it must be winter, but there was no snow on the ground. I was cold and frightened. I felt all alone, and was desperate to be away from this dark place. Suddenly, I felt a presence nearby and a voice said, "Here, pilgrim, take my hand." And I was led into the light.

Many of us, at one time or another, have had this kind of dream. We are in the dark and someone brings illumination. We are frightened and someone comforts us. We are lost and someone guides us.

And in the daylight, after the dream has vanished, we all still need a guide every now and then. All through our lives we need help and understanding and guidance. If we're lucky, the guide finds us.

So it was with my friend Mary, a nurse, who took me on a journey that led me through the darkest part of the forest into the light we call Life.

Sitting together in the hospital cafeteria, sipping coffee and laughing about the children, Mary turned suddenly serious.

"Time for you to be movin' on, manchild," she said. "Time to do the real work God set you down here for." She placed her hand over mine and I looked down at her thick, powerful fingers as they intertwined mine. Her skin as black as mine is white. I looked into her eyes wondering what she meant.

"Lots more for you to be doin', and time slippin' by. Time for you to move up the ladder."

"What do you mean, Mary?"

"You been doin' child's play, honey," she smiled broadly and patted my hand. But time's come to move on and do some hard work. I think you're ready. I been watchin' you."

"What kind of work?"

"I think you should move up to the terminal ward and work with those children." She held my hand tightly.

I felt my stomach knot up and I was sure that beads of sweat had formed on my brow. I had a hard time with children who were bedridden and couldn't get up to play with the others. The thought of working with children who were dying seemed beyond my ability.

But, in the end, Mary convinced me. Just like she always did.

WHERE IS HEAVEN?

K A T H Y

I woke up to the sound of rain beating on my window.
I rolled over, hugged my pillow, and tried to find my way back
to the dream I was having. "Tap, tap, tap," went the raindrops
against the glass, and I knew that my dream would have
to wait.

Two hours later, I shook off the raindrops like an old hound
dog, and set off down the hospital corridor in search of Mary.

I peeked into one room after another, saying hello to familiar
faces, and asking where the elusive Miss Mary might be.

I found her tucking in the covers around a very frightened-
looking little girl.

"Good morning, Miss Mary. Lovely day today," I smiled.

She turned and gave me the evil eye. "Don' you be givin' me
that sweet talk, Mister Silly, we got serious problems right here,
right now. Say hi to Kathy, my newest guest."

"I think Kathy feels more like your prisoner. If you tuck her
in any tighter I can bounce a quarter off her tummy."

Kathy giggled.

"Das right, fool, make the child laugh. I got better things to do than be part of your silliness." She winked and swept out the door with all the grace of a Sherman tank.

"Well," I said sitting down on the side of her bed. "What's the plan?"

"Huh?" replied Kathy.

"We have to have a plan, kiddo, if we're going to have any fun. Nothing really good ever happens without a plan. So, what is it?"

"I don't know. I'm sick," she replied in a small voice.

"OK, let's plan to get better."

"I can't. I'm terminal." Her lip trembled.

"Well then let's make a plan to *feel* better." I smiled at her but she didn't smile back.

"Why?"

"Why *what*?" I returned.

"Why plan to feel better if you're gonna die?"

"How soon are you leaving?" I asked.

"Six months—maybe."

"Well that's plenty of time to make plans and do all sorts of things."

"Why?"

"Why *not*?" I winked at her but she still wasn't smiling.

"What's the name on your ticket?" I asked.

"I don't know what you mean," she replied.

"What's the name of the disease that's giving you a ticket to heaven?"

"Cancer," she replied without any hint of emotion.

"Are you here for chemo?"

"Yes."

"Have you met the Eggheads, yet?"

"Who?" she asked, clearly confused.

"The Eggheads—a very special gang of kids who belong to this very, very exclusive club. The initiation is taking chemo."

"That's gross," replied Kathy.

"Totally," I responded. "Wait here, I'll round them up."

A few minutes later I returned with my band of baldies, and they surrounded Kathy's bed and bombarded her with greetings and questions.

"I'm fourteen too!" squealed Lisa. "Isn't it gross?"

"Where are you from?"

"What school do you go to?"

"Who's your doctor?"

"What's your timetable?"

"Can she come to Harmony, Bear? Please?" begged Lisa.

"What's Harmony?" asked Kathy.

"It's the best!" replied Bobby. "We do all this great stuff together and we talk things over and we get in people's faces."

"What?" responded Kathy.

"We do the *Rocky* thing, you know, like *down* but not *out*. We walk tall. We strut like Robert and we get in people's faces and we let 'em know we are definitely A-L-I-V-E in capital letters."

"But aren't you all—terminal?"

"Sure. But so what? Everybody is gonna check out sooner or later. No major deal about that. You have to make a plan and get with the program or else you waste time, you waste life. Like the Fuzzy One here says, ya gotta hit the dawn and kick butt or you're not in the game. Right Mister Silly?"

"Right, Bobby."

"So, Kathy, what's the plan?" asks Robert.

"I guess you'll have to teach me to strut," she replied with a small smile.

H A R M O N Y

In the beginning, more than twelve years ago, I bungled my way through everything. No one was doing what I was doing. There were plenty of people working with terminally ill patients both young and old, but their focus was different from mine. I was looking for a way for people who loved each other to say goodbye, and "it was great being with you in the time we had." I read all the books I could find. Mostly they were by professionals writing for other professionals. Plain

folk, like me, without any initials after our names, were
on our own.

So I stumbled around, telling stories, making children and
old people laugh. I rocked babies, read to the blind, wrote letters
for the infirm, and tried to be useful.

I listened. And I learned from the greatest teachers of all, the
patients themselves. They pointed the direction, and we hacked
through the red tape and underbrush until we found a clearing
in the woods. I called it Harmony.

Harmony is a place where we come together to gather our
thoughts and feelings, like wild flowers in a field. It is a space in
our minds, but it is more than that—it is quiet and serene and
beautiful and, most importantly, safe. It is what we, the group,
make it. But each person shapes it differently.

We have a few rituals, and a few ceremonies, plus a few rules,
but nothing elaborate. In the mystical tradition of King Arthur's
round table, we sit in a circle so that no one has a better position
than anyone else. We hold hands because it is friendly, and
because it lets us feel joined. We breathe deeply because it's good
for us and it feels good—it's calming. We get quiet for the same
reasons.

We hug a lot. We laugh a lot. Sometimes we sing, but not
too often. We try to be truthful, and when we aren't we hope
that someone will have the courage to tell us so that we can
get straight.

One of the tiny rules in Harmony is that no one can be judgmental. Everyone has an equal right to be foolish. Even silly, like me.

And we cry.

The children like Harmony because it can be magical. They can be anything and anyone they want to be, and it's OK. In fact, one of the best things about Harmony is that almost everything is OK. Even anger. Even depression. Even fear. We deal with everything by facing it straight on.

Over the years the children have taught me that nothing is too serious or too silly to talk about. If they say it's important, it is. That is the foundation of their wisdom. They still believe in magic and princes hidden inside beasts. It is how they find life in the face of death.

Here is a list from Harmony. It might, at first glance, appear to be a silly list of why things (not people) die. But how silly is it, really?

1. Because they got old. (dogs)
2. Because they faded. (jeans)
3. Because they got used up. (liquid detergent)
4. Because they got replaced. (tires)
5. Because it was their season. (plants)
6. Because they expired. (discount coupons)
7. Because they weren't needed. (crutches)
8. Because they were forgotten. (toys)

9. Because I outgrew them. (shoes)

10. Because something better came out. (car)

Looking over this list you might get the idea that things and people aren't so different. I've met a lot of dying people who might have given several of these reasons for their own approaching end.

Children, on the other hand, are not quite so cynical. Amazingly, they seem to understand the simple concept that they are dying because they are dying. They have a disease that may be winning the battle for their life, and they accept that.

It doesn't mean they don't fight. In fact they are all terrific warriors. It is just that children are better at the simple truth than adults are. They deny less and accept more.

And that makes Harmony more harmonious.

S I D D L Y

Sidney, a.k.a. "Siddly," is a longtime survivor. He is seven, and was born with full-blown AIDS. He has survived with a smile, and a lisp, and the delightful ability to mispronounce words, including his own name. He is the clown in the group, my apprentice, a Mister Silly Junior. He is Siddly the Magnificent.

"I whoosh I wooden be dying," announces Siddly. "But that's what the dockers tell me I'm doing, so I guest I better do it wite."

"Doing it right" is a popular concept with these kids, and with a few adults I've met as well.

"What exactly is *the right way*, Siddly?" I inquire.

"Well," he replies with a knitted brow and sparking brown eyes. "Let me shee if I can 'splain that. I believe that the wite way to die is wif a full plate."

Everyone laughs. This refers to my philosophy as taught by Patrick Dennis's outrageous character, Auntie Mame, that, "Life is a banquet and most fools are starving to death." Kids love the idea.

"I want to fill up my plate wif life every day, s'wen Mishta Def comes, I'll have plenty to share wif him."

"You want to give Mister Death some life off your plate?"

"Sure. I think if he got a weely good taste of life, he'd want some more, and then some more, and he'd forget about me. He'd want to live too, because life's so 'licious." He giggles, and everyone joins in.

Siddly's recipe for life—for living longer: Take an extra helping of life's rich banquet, because Mister Death may be dropping by—and just maybe we can tempt him with a donut or two.

I think Siddly is going to make an excellent Court Jester.

C L O W N I N G

When I started working with kids I had no special identity. I wasn't a doctor or a nurse or a therapist or analyst or any of the other characters that entered their daily lives. I was just a man who brought them bears and told them stories and made them laugh. To some I was Ted. To others I was The Bear Man or just Bear.

In the world beyond the pale green walls, I was an artist, an author, an off-Broadway actor/director/writer/producer, a mural painter, a puppeteer, and last but not least, a teddy bear maker. I have often commented that the inscription on my tombstone will read: "It seemed like a good idea at the time."

In time, I may become a butcher, a baker, and a candlestick maker. I like change. I'm a Gemini. That's either an explanation or an excuse depending on your point of view.

We all search for our identity. But one day I got tired of searching, and settled for just accepting myself as I am. I let other people identify me. My friend Sarah loves me because I can wear so many different hats at her dinner parties. I fill in when one of her "identities" cancels. I can be "Author" or "Artist" or "Mr. Whateversheneeds."

In time my true identity emerged, thanks to a serious young man of six years named Jason.

In and out of hospitals since the day he was born, Jason had seen it all—and was having none of it. He called himself "the human pincushion" and bragged that he'd been stuck with more needles than any other child in the room. Needles are the villains in all hospitalized children's lives, and no one argued with Jason. He thought it was all a drag, and told us so. He stood, back turned to us, looking out the window.

We went on without him. We played our games, told our stories and hugged our bears. At the end of the day he pronounced me silly.

"You're silly!" he shouted at me. "You and your bear are silly." His face screwed up into a mask of hostility. "You're just a Mister Silly and your dumb ol' bear is silly too."

In time, Jason's anger gave way to acceptance and friendship, but his name for me stuck fast, and I became Mister Silly to everyone.

I wasn't sure I liked it at first. But then I remembered that in the days of King Arthur only two people could tell the king the absolute truth without fear of reprisal—Merlin, the wizard, and the Court Jester, the fool. I wasn't clever enough to be a wizard but I was foolish enough to be the jester. And I laughed out loud at my new identity— Mister Silly.

A wise old teddy bear once remarked that "life is a circus with too few clowns." I believe that's true. It seems to me that there are far too many lions and tigers and bears in the circus of life, and not nearly enough clowns falling down. Life needs a pie in the face every now and then, and a good clown can really get the job done.

Working with terminal children, I quickly learned how little laughter was being prescribed by their physicians. In my role as Mister Silly, D.L. (Doctor of Laughter) I could increase their daily dosage.

I have long believed that laughter is a bridge as well as a balm. They are children and I am a grownup. They are terminal and I am not. Laughter allows us to meet halfway.

Over the years the children have taught me how to deal better with the coming event of death. And they have asked me to help their parents understand their need for truth and honesty.

Sometimes we sit in a circle and make tape recordings to send home, and we write letters that we may never send but need to write. We write a Last Will and Testament, because they have a legacy to leave behind. I have learned not to treat them any differently than dying adults—because their needs and wishes are the same.

Sometimes I am their go-between or their advocate in the world of adults. Time and again I am the lab rat that they test in the labyrinth and examine for clarification of their ideas about how these strange creatures—adults—behave. I am their crying towel, and their security blanket. Sometimes a hero and sometimes a slave. For Mister Silly, it is all in a day's work.

If you think you'd like to join the Mister Silly School of Clowning and Compassion, see if you can answer these questions:

1. When I die, will I go to heaven?
2. Where is heaven, and does it have a baseball field?
3. When my doll died, did she go to heaven?
4. Why won't my mommy cry?
5. Is Mickey Mouse a saint?

6. Will it hurt when I die?

7. Is the Terminator the angel of death?

8. Are angels boys or girls?

9. Can I choose what I come back as next time? I don't want to be a girl again.

10. What color is God?

In the Quiz of Life there are no easy answers, but we have a built-in textbook in our hearts, and that's always where the best answers come from.

Answer with the heart.

J A N E

Another sweltering summer day in the city. We are sitting together in the park, trying to cool off in a bit of shade. What an odd assortment we must appear to be— half-a-dozen bald children and a six-foot-five old man with white hair and a beard. Am I the Pied Piper of Harmony, I wonder? Or just Mister Silly and his merry band of eggheads?

We are all drinking water from plastic bottles and mopping sweat from our brows. The sunlight dances in the moisture on the children's heads and they seem to be bathed in glistening light.

"Did you know that Sarah passed away?" asks Jane.

"No," I reply. "I didn't."

"Sarah *died*, Jane," says Connie, who is fourteen. "She didn't pass away like a whiff of smoke, and she didn't cross over to the other side like a jaywalker. She died. She is dead. Say it, Jane."

"Shut up, Connie. I don't like to say that. You know it makes me sad to say that," cries Jane, who is nine.

"This is Harmony, Jane. This is where we say the truth. You can pretend all you want anywhere else, but not here. Say 'Sarah died.' Say it now."

"Sarah died," mumbles Jane.

"Why are you so mean to Jane?" Timmy asks.

"Am I being mean, Bear?" she asks, looking straight at me.

"Depends on why you want Jane to say it. Why is it so important that she say those particular words?" I ask.

"I can't believe you are asking that when *you're* the one who says that using other words for things is a deception and we shouldn't do it."

"True. But maybe Jane needs those words right now, like a crutch to hop on until she heals a little." I look over at Jane, who is crying softly.

"No good," replies Connie. "That's a cop-out. Jane has had plenty of time to get used to the idea that Sarah was going to die. She's just in denial."

"That fancy word is a no-no here, Connie. It's as untruthful as 'passed away.' Say what you mean."

"Jane can't—or won't—face her own death, so she avoids the word. She doesn't want to die, so she says that Sarah passed away, and makes it sound like a vacation or something. It's like saying that cancer is an inconvenience instead of a killer disease."

"Good point, but I want to know why it bothers you so much today?"

"It bothers me because I loved Sarah too, and I miss her just as much as Jane does. But I refuse to pretend that she isn't dead. That she simply crossed over to the other side. She's dead and she's gone and I have to face that and so does Jane."

"Maybe Jane isn't ready for that yet," I suggest.

"Well, I need her to be!" cries Connie. "I need her to be my friend and be realistic so we can grieve together. I need her to help me miss Sarah and remember her with me. I need Jane to be strong too because I can't really do it alone."

"Oh, Connie, I'm so sorry . . ." cries Jane, hugging her friend.

We sit quietly for a moment, and then I suggest that we do an honoring closure for Sarah. Saying goodbye is never easy, but remembering and honoring sometimes ease the pain.

One of the ways we do this is to go around the circle and think of a word or a phrase that is the key to our memory of our loved one. This is a kind of short-form memorial service, where people get up and give a full-length honoring remembrance. By using just one word, I find that we get to a deeper feeling that is very special and personal and doesn't need to be explained to or understood by the rest of the group. We do this at the end of every Harmony session, but usually it is for our own special person that we are thinking of at the moment. Today we are all going to do it for Sarah.

I begin. "Pumpkins."

"July 4th last year," says Connie.

"Elvis."

"Cream cheese."

"Rocky Horror Picture Show."

"Seashells."

"Fireworks."

"Virginity." (giggles)

"Beating the odds."

"Bear," asks Jane, after it is over, "Can we do balloons next week for Sarah?"

"Sure. Shall we do white, or colors?" I ask.

"Colors, please. Sarah loved colors."

The following week we do the balloons. This is a ceremony that I believe began as a remembrance to honor people who had died of AIDS. It is a simple ceremony, like the one-word remembrance. The balloons symbolize letting go of your loved one. So we simply stand in a circle, and think about Sarah, and when we accept her death in our hearts and minds, we let go of the balloons.

"There is only one rule," Mary explained to me when I began working with terminal children. "Never lie to them. Always tell the truth—no matter what!"

At the time it seemed simple enough, but I quickly learned that it was far from easy. The truth is often hard to find. Here are a few examples of their questions to show you what I mean:

"Am I going to die?"

"Who is God?"

"Why won't my daddy visit me?"

"Is the Doctor mad at me? Is that why he hurts me?"

"Who is Death?"

"Where is Heaven?"

What are the truthful answers to those questions? At first they seemed impossible to answer, but over the years the children have taught me. Not all of the answers are easy, or the same, but they all have a way of being the truth—if only for a moment.

"Am I going to die?"

Yes, we all are going to die because that is simply what happens to us. Sooner or later, everything that lives will die. The real question is "When?"

The answer to that isn't easy, but it is simple—"When your season ends and your time comes. Just like the flowers in the field."

"Who is God?"

God reveals himself differently to each person. Some people find God in a church. Others find God in a temple or a mosque or a tree. But the truth is that God is always found in your own heart, and that is the best place to look.

"Why won't my daddy visit me?"

Sometimes Daddy is more frightened of death than you are and you must help him not to be afraid. Daddy is afraid because he loves you and doesn't want you to go away—doesn't want you to die.

"Is the Doctor mad at me? Is that why he hurts me?"

No, the Doctor cares for you very much and it hurts him to see you in pain. He wants to help you. That's why he became a doctor but it isn't always easy, and some of the tools he uses to make you better are painful, but they are not a punishment.

"Who is Death?"

My dear grandmother always said that death was the fellow who asked you for the last waltz—the final dance of life. He's not the boogeyman. He's just a guy with a difficult job.

"Where is heaven?"

Turn left at your wishes and turn right at your dreams—heaven is just beyond that.

There are those who would argue that the subtle difference between truth and honesty is that truth comes from the brain and honesty from the heart. This sort of discussion seems point-less when I examine the harsh reality of working with children who face death.

Truth is a gift that often comes strangely wrapped. Sometimes in a plain brown wrapper. At other times, it arrives with a pretty bow. Tough truth, it seems, needs a bit of dressing up.

But plainly-wrapped or with a bow, the truth is always better than a lie. Lying stinks, and kids have a great sense of smell.

So when kids ask a really impossible question, I square my shoulders, stick out my chin and reply with the ultimate truth.

"I don't know."

W A L L Y

The brilliant sun filtered through the leaves overhead and cast intricate, lacy patterns across the grass. We had spread out several blankets and were sitting in a circle, cross-legged, holding hands, eyes closed, breathing deeply, and finding our *center*.

This is my own version of yoga, but I find that it calms everyone down and gets us all to focus. Getting children to focus isn't too easy—they are naturally interrupted by the slightest diversion.

"Is everyone in Harmony?" I ask. They respond that they are and we begin.

"Does someone named Amy have a question?" I ask, trying to get the ball rolling.

"Is death a punishment?" asks Amy, who is nine.

"What do you think?" I ask her.

"I heard my aunt say that death was God's punishment for our wickedness and transgressions."

"What are transgressions?" asks Wally, who is seven.

"Mortal sins," offers Tommy, who, at twelve, is the oldest member of this group and a self-appointed know-it-all.

"I don't believe in sin," offers Mary, nine.

"Doesn't matter," replies Tommy, "God *does!*"

"Is that true, Mister Silly?" asks Wally.

"Well, yes and no. The Bible talks about sin but it also talks about forgiveness. Sin is a bad thing you do, but if you say you're sorry then you can be forgiven. The important thing to remember is that the Bible says that everyone does bad things sometimes, but they can always be forgiven."

"If I don't say I'm sorry will I still be forgiven?" asks Wally, openly concerned.

"Why wouldn't you say you're sorry?" I ask.

"Well, maybe I don't think what I did was wicked," he replies.

"Can you explain that better for us?" I ask.

"Well, I have AIDS and I'm gonna die, but I don't think I did anything wrong. So will I be forgiven or will I burn in hell like my aunt says?"

"No, Wally, you won't burn in hell, and you're absolutely right when you say you didn't do anything wrong. Death is not a punishment. Death is what happens at the end of our life's journey—that's all. Everything dies. Everything."

"Will I feel anything when they bury me?" asks Wally.

"Wally, after you die you won't feel anything, so you'll be perfectly safe buried in the ground. Look at all the things that live under the ground—all the plants and bugs and small animals, and even some pretty big ones like woodchucks. There's nothing to be afraid of."

"But I won't be able to breathe under the ground," Wally persisted.

"You only need to breathe to be alive. After you die you don't need to. That's the big difference."

"Are you sure?"

"Yes." I reply. "Scout's honor."

"OK."

Wally had a lot more questions about death and the process we call dying. In time, he and the others came to their own understanding and acceptance of that process, but not before they asked another hundred questions.

Answering questions, no matter how silly they seem, is like kissing a boo-boo—it takes the fear and the pain away for a moment.

Answers, like the truth, are a night light that keeps the boogeyman away.

Or maybe they are like a patchwork quilt in which each answer is like a brightly colored square of fabric that is stitched together to become something we can wrap ourselves in, and be comforted.

W H Y

If you have ever spent much time around little kids, you know that their favorite question is why.

"Why is the sky blue?"

"Why does my tummy make noises?"

"Why are girls dumb?"

"Why are boys dumb?"

On and on and until finally, the ultimate question: "Am I going to die?"

Yes.

We all are going to die.

"Why?"

Because that is what all living things do, they die.

Amazingly, children accept this truth better than adults do. If you show a child how a flower blooms, flourishes, and then dies, they get it. For some reason, as we get older, we want more complicated reasons for everything. Even those things that are as plain as the nose on your face.

When asked "Am I going to die?" and given the answer "Yes," a child will follow with a barrage of other questions.

"Will I go to heaven?" "Will you miss me?" "Will I meet God?" "Will I be an angel?" "Will I remember being alive on Earth?" "What if I was naughty, will I still go to heaven?" and, of course, "Why do I have to die?"

There are no easy answers to any of these questions, but a nice trick that I learned from every Freudian analyst who ever owned a leather couch is to turn the question back on the asker: "What do you think?"

While adults don't often fall prey to this ploy, it works very well with children, who have ideas about everything and the energy to tell you if you have the patience to listen.

Like the patient on the couch who asks his doctor if he is being neurotic when he already knows the answer—or he wouldn't be paying a hundred bucks to ask—the children aren't so much seeking new answers as confirmation of what they already believe.

Now, I believe that the answers to most questions are within the questions themselves.

In my other books I show how this works; when people ask, "What can I do?" I suggest that they answer their own question with their own words rearranged: "Do what I can."

When a child (or even an adult) asks, "Will I go to heaven?" the answer they want is inside the question and is made up of the same exact words: "I will go to heaven."

"Will I meet God?" becomes "I will meet God."

"Will I be an angel?" becomes "I will be an angel."

Of course, it isn't always that simple, but if you don't complicate simple questions you will have more time and energy to deal with the difficult and tricky ones. In the end, many of the questions about death deal with a far greater question, the question of faith.

I am not talking about the faith associated with religion, and the concept of a higher being, but of faith in the process of death. There are so many questions that can only be answered with the word "because." "Because that is the process and that is the way it works." Accepting *the process* as an answer is a very difficult thing for anyone, young or old, to do. But it is far better to try to comfort someone with that idea than with some euphemism that is easier to say but in reality is far more dangerous.

For example, no one can tell us why Daddy died. They can tell us how—A heart attack. Cancer. A car crash. But that is how, not why. But some adults might tell children, "God took Daddy to heaven," thinking that this will comfort the child. Not so. In fact, it might make the child angry with God for taking Daddy. Care must be taken not to confuse children—or adults—about the truth of what is happening. Deception, misdirection, and avoidance are like quicksand—the more you struggle, the deeper you sink.

Children love fantasy, but when they ask a question, they want a truthful answer. I have never met a child who didn't.

C O O K I E

There is a silence when the snow falls that is like no other. No matter the time of day, the hush that the falling crystals bring is unique, as unique as the flakes themselves.

Sometimes, when I am feeling poetic, I think of the children as snowflakes—seemingly alike but, in reality, completely different.

When Charles, a.k.a. "Cookie," joined our group, he had nothing to say. When I'd ask what he was thinking about he'd reply:

"Nuttin'."

"And what are you feeling?"

"Nuttin'."

"Then what do you want to do?"

"Nuttin'."

Listening to Cookie was like listening to the snow—more sight than sound. So like a deaf person, I began to listen with my eyes.

When others made comments I watched for Cookie's face to tell me what he was thinking and feeling. Soon I could read his responses like words on a page. He would wince or frown or grin or scowl as others spoke their thoughts. In time, I heard his voice, even though he remained silent.

At ten, Cookie faced the prospect of death with a shield of steely silence. His armor and weapons were forged in quiet. I began to believe that he thought that if he stayed perfectly still, Death would not notice him and pass him by. In this way he was like a rabbit in the road with a truck bearing down full throttle. I wanted to warn him, but I was afraid to startle him, to disarm him and leave him defenseless.

The children were less cautious.

"I don't know why you even bother to come here, Cookie, you never say anything about anything to anyone," said Rebecca.

Rebecca was a self-appointed spokesperson for everything and everyone.

"You talk 'nough for everyone," replied Cookie.

"I'm just trying to get you to open up," she responded, folding her hands primly in her lap.

"Ferget it. I ain't no can that hasta be opened up. My deal is listenin' and watchin'. Just like Mista Silly. He's always watchin'."

Oops. Caught.

"Does that bother you?" I asked.

"Naw. It's yer thing I guess," he shrugged. "Yer thing is to git us ta talk 'bout dyin'. OK. It sucks. The end."

"There's more to it than that," I suggested.

"Sure, the long version. I just cut to the basics. Hello. Goodbye." He frowned a minute, and then seemed pleased with himself.

"What about the in-between?" I asked.

"What about it?" he asked me back with a shrug of his shoulders.

"Well, there's here and now and tomorrow and the day after that."

"Yeah, well my book is a short read, ya know. I ain't gonna be around long enough to fill more 'n a few pages."

"OK, so you're not going to be around long enough to be a great big thick novel like *War and Peace* but you might be enough for a very good short story."

"Yeah, *The Life and Death of Cookie*. I was born. I lived an' then I died. You can put it all on a index card."

"Cookie, the truth is that everyone can compress their lives into the size of an index card. Some very, very important people who do wonderful things die and their whole life is reduced to a paragraph in the obituaries. For that matter, most people's lives are condensed to a few lines on their tombstone. But that's what other people say about them, not what they say about themselves. Some writers have devoted pages and pages of words describing a single moment in their life.

"It isn't how long you live, it's how much you live."

"You finished?" he asked.

"Maybe," I replied.

"Ya know what my nickname stands fer?"

"Let me guess. Tough cookie. Right?" I smiled.

"Hundert percent. I was inna gang. I did good fer myself. I had rep. Then this stuff happens and they tell me I gotta fight to stay well. So I do. Then they say I'm losin' the fight—I'm gonna die. Jes like that. It messed me up. I wanted to fight. I woulda fought wit everythin' I had but the odds were stacked against me. I was marked a loser by the Big Guy. So I figger why push it, and I shut up. All this talkin' ain't gonna get me another day."

"Are we supposed to feel sorry for you?" asked Rebecca.

"No."

"Good, because we don't—and least I don't. But I guess we all feel the same way. Death sucks, but we have no choice about it so I think it's better to talk about what we feel and what we think than to keep it all inside. It won't change the fact that we're dying but it could change the fact that right now we're living."

I watched Cookie's face change expression as Rebecca's words assaulted him. When she stopped talking I watched him process it. Then he turned and looked at me.

"Watcha see, Mista Silly?"

"I saw you listening, and I saw you answering, and I saw you agreeing."

"You got good eyes," he winked.

I winked back.

L I S T E N I N G

Listening is the hardest thing we are asked to do. Americans spend millions of hours watching (and listening) to talk shows where the hosts talk more than the guests—where, in fact, the *audience* talks more than the guests. That's probably why they're called talk shows, nobody listens.

Think about your everyday conversations at home and at work. Think about how you listen to other people. Are you really hearing them, or are you already thinking about what you're going to say next? I'll bet it's the latter more than the former.

Each decade or so we get a whole new batch of what are now called "buzz words." These are the boldface words of speech. They used to be called "catch phrases" a few years ago. Companies with product to sell used to call them slogans.

One of today's buzz words is FOCUS.

Athletes *focus* on the difficult aspects of their sport. Observers in the media now *focus* where they used to spotlight, highlight, and pinpoint.

When I was growing up they only thing I used to *focus* was my camera. As I peered through my lens, all I saw at first was a blurred image. Then, as I twisted the lens, the image came into focus. Right in the center of my lens was a tiny circle, which was used to achieve the clearest possible picture. If that tiny circle was perfectly sharp, the rest of the area would be just as clear.

When it is our time to listen, we need to focus in that tiny circle in order to make the entire picture clear and sharp and detailed.

In *Gentle Closings* I wrote about aggressive listening, and how important it is to listen 100% to the words and wishes of the dying. We must wipe our slates clean and let the speakers write their words on a fresh, uncluttered surface. We must literally absorb all we hear, like a kitchen sponge. Only then can we really hear the voices of our loved ones.

R O B I N

Snow blankets the city and is still falling when we form our morning circle in Harmony. This is the first snow that Robin has ever seen, because she grew up in Florida. Now, at twelve, she is here for her first series of chemo. Around her the Eggheads are like a reflection in her mind's mirror. She, too, will probably lose her hair and join the ranks of the Eggheads.

Eggheads is what they call themselves. No one else is allowed to use that name. It is a closed society, and you must be born into it.

When we started these meetings they all wore caps and scarves to make it easier on me—and themselves. Embarrass ment is a badge others make them wear. I persuaded them to use their baldness as another kind of badge. A badge of honor for their valiant effort not just to survive but to win against the odds.

I explained all this to Robin as she sat with us and listened as we talked about death, and dying, and being alive.

"This is my third series of chemo," said Bobby, who is nine.

"I've been in remission, but the cancer keeps coming back. Last year I went to Paul Newman's camp. It was great, and I made a lot of friends. More Eggheads. We write to each other and compare notes. Sometimes I don't like being in the outside world because . . . because I'm not really like *them*, and I want to be. When I'm here I feel OK. I feel normal. But out there I'm— you know, different."

"A freak," remarks Tommy, who is twelve.

"Yeah."

"I just want to be normal again," responds Sallie, who is fourteen. "I want long golden curls and be the prom queen and have dates and make out with boys."

Giggles, all around.

"Hey, be the Sinead O'Connor of your high school," replies Robert, who is sixteen. "Yo, girl, do your thing and don't be lettin' those fools bring you down. Most of my friends are shavin' their heads right now 'cause it's the thing."

"Listen, Robert, that's OK for you and your homeboys, but my family lives in uptight Westchester and there are no bald prom queens."

"Girl, be a trendsetter. Get your act together and SHOW them. Kick ass, bitch. Don' let them get you down. And if they do that, then split. We don' have TIME, babycakes. Don' be fussin' with that silliness—STRUT!"

"Come on, Robert, don't give me your street-boy attitude about this. I'm not totally serious about being prom queen but I am totally serious about being normal again."

"Ain't never gonna be, girl. Mostly we all gonna die in a few years. I am for sure. AIDS is real final, you know. But I'm not sittin' still for it. I'm workin' the street."

"What does that mean?" asks Robin, speaking for the first time.

"Welcome aboard," smiles Robert, broadly.

"What it means, pretty birdgirl, is that I am dancing as fast as my feet will carry me. It means I'm up bright and early and out on the street of life—lookin' and livin'. And every night I get on my knees and thank Jesus for that day and claim my right to have another. It means what my man here calls 'honoring the day,' and claimin' it for myself. It means I'm dyin', BUT, I ain't dead yet."

"I wish I had your courage," said Robin. "I feel defeated before I've begun. I had so many real dreams that I wanted. Even before I got sick I felt different. I loved to read. Hated TV. I'd rather make my own clothes than go to the GAP. When I got diagnosed I thought to myself, well, that's it. It's over."

"Ain't over till it's over, girl."

"Easy for you to say, you seem to have the kind of fighting spirit that I don't," sighed Robin.

"Birdgirl, I'm a product of the projects. I can talk street or I can talk straight. I use the language of the moment 'cause I have to live in the moment. But I read books, and I don't shop the GAP either. I do the thrifts and flea markets for vintage. I'm a vintage man, you know."

"We're different."

"We the same, Robin. We dyin'."

DREAMS

I guess we all have dreams, and I guess we all pretty much accept the idea that they have some meaning. The living and the dying both dream about life and death—they have dreams of falling, or sinking, or flying, or laughing, or a host of other terrors and joys.

Some dreams are illuminations, or premonitions of what the future may bring. And some dreams are wishes that may or may not come true.

The unemployed dream of finding a new job. The sick dream of being healed. The widow dreams of finding a new partner, and the child whose mother dies dreams of finding a new parent. The old remember what was, and dream of what might be again. And the young imagine the future, and dream of what will be.

When a child is denied that dream, it may seem like a nightmare. But a child's life may be a shooting star—one brief shining moment crossing the landscape of our life, a moment brilliant in beauty but brief in duration. Children are filled with joy and laughter, and their final gift to us is the gift of life—their life. In facing death, they show us how to live.

Children are everything that life has to offer. They *are* the dream.

And even after they are gone, the dream lives on.

R U S T Y

The first buds of spring popped out along the branches of trees in Central Park. There was still a slight chill in the air, and as I sipped coffee from a Styrofoam cup I wondered if I would be able to take the kids outdoors today. I hoped we could, because it always lifted their spirits to be outside, away from the pale green walls. I still had forty-five minutes before I could go upstairs, and I thought about what this day might bring.

"May we talk about heaven today, Mister Silly?" asks Rusty, who is a very old seven. "Please?"

"What about heaven?" I ask.

"Where is it?"

"Well, you know that nobody has ever come back to tell us that, so we don't know for sure."

"My mother says heaven is up in the sky where God is, but I wonder why everyone doesn't fall out of the clouds back down to Earth."

"Because after you die you're just a spirit with no body. You just float around," says Timmy, who is four.

"If I'm just a spirit, how will my mother find me when she comes to heaven?"

"They all wear name tags," jokes Sandy, sixteen.

"Do they, Mister Silly?" asks Rusty.

"No, they don't. Sandy is just being a jerk."

(laughter)

"Why all these questions about heaven, Rusty?" I ask.

"My roommate died last night, and I heard the priest tell his parents that he was at peace now, in heaven. I wondered where it really was and how he got there."

"Anyone want to answer that?" I wonder aloud.

"My mother says that there is no heaven," announces Nancy, ten. "She says that heaven is in the hearts of everyone who loves you, so when you die you go to live in their hearts."

"Sounds like a tight squeeze to me," quips Sandy.

"Cool it, Sandy. If you haven't anything honest to say then keep quiet. Your little jokes are just a defense against what scares you, and everyone here knows that. Harmony is no place for pretending. Now, why don't you tell us why this conversation upsets you—really." I lean back and wait with the others for his response.

"He's out of remission," says Connie flatly.

"I AM NOT!" shouts Sandy.

"Are too," says Connie quietly.

"Are you?" I ask.

"Yeah."

We all sit together quietly for a moment, considering how we feel about this news—what we all fear for one another. Remission is a step away from death. Coming out of remission is a step backward—closer to possible death. Remission is even harder to talk about than death. It is more real to them all. Death is still an unknown abstraction.

"Are you afraid to die?" asks Rusty.

"Everyone is afraid to die," replies Sandy.

"Is that true, Mister Silly?" asks Rusty.

"Well, maybe. I think we *are* all afraid to die, but that fear is different for everyone.

"There is the basic fear of anything unknown. That fear is like going into a strange, dark room. We know there isn't really a boogeyman in the room, but there are things in there that we don't know about. We might fall over a chair, or bump into a table and stub our toe. So we hesitate because of the unknown, and we call that fear. But if we turn the light on and see what's really in the room, then we don't need to hesitate and we lose that fear.

"People fear death in different ways. In Norway, for instance, back when the Vikings roamed the seas, they feared death only if they died without honor. If they died with honor they went to Valhalla, which was their heaven. In Japan they also fear death without honor, and here in the United States, some Native

Americans believe that death with honor brings you straight to the happy hunting grounds—their idea of heaven."

"What is honor, Mister Silly?"

"Honor—is being true to yourself and what you believe. And honor is treating other people with respect and love."

"Like the Golden Rule," says Timmy.

"Yes."

"But where is heaven?" persists Rusty.

"Well, *I* think that heaven is where you want it to be. It is in your mother's heart, or up in the sky, or with the Vikings in Valhalla or out on the Montana plains with the buffalo. I was sitting next to a lady in a restaurant last week and after she tasted her soup she exclaimed: 'This is heaven, darling.' Who knows? That might be her idea of heaven.

"It doesn't really matter where I think it is or where Sandy thinks it is, or Connie or Timmy or any of your parents. I think it's important for you to decide where *you* want it to be, so when you do die you'll know exactly where you are going.

"It's important not to be afraid that death and heaven are like that dark room where we stumble over things. It's better to think of heaven as a place you want to be, where the lights are on and you can see where everything is. Then maybe it won't be so scary."

"Maybe it's like the snowflakes," said Rusty. "Like you said, Mr. Silly, every life is different, and every death is different for each of us. So maybe every heaven is different too."

"I like that idea, Rusty." I said, smiling. "I just hope my heaven has a beach."

CONFRONTATION

In *Gentle Closings* I told the story about the bunny and the Eggheads. In that adventure, I dressed up in the most outrageously grotesque pink bunny costume I could find, went to the hospital on Easter morning, and painted the children's bald heads like Easter eggs. *They* were delighted, but the doctors and nurses were horrified. So were their parents.

Being chastised by a bunch of uptight, self-conscious adults was nothing compared to the delighted screams of joy the children gave as each new color was applied to their hairless heads.

Laughter is the light that illuminates even the darkest moments, chases the shadows away, and keeps Mister Death in the corner.

And laughter is a sword and a shield that lets us do battle with an enemy so enormous that we cannot comprehend it. In this life and death battle, confrontation is the name of the game. Truth is the only rule. Hitting things square and head-on is the tactic. We don't have time for subtle maneuvers.

Each child does battle in a different way, and it is important to let them work out the strategy on their own. Children need affirmation of their ideas, no matter how silly they may seem to adults or even to one another. I learned that no matter how outlandish their ideas might seem on the surface, there is a wisdom beneath them that is brilliant.

Sharon wanted Lassie to be the one to take her to heaven. When one of the boys chided her by saying that Lassie was only a dog, Sharon responded, "I know *that*, but Lassie always knows how to get back home." Why trust an angel you never met when you can have a sure thing like Lassie? Makes perfect sense to me.

Children want answers, but it isn't always easy to determine how much of an answer they really want. So I try to get them to answer their own questions. Most of their questions about death and dying are grounded in a basic fear of the unknown. Death as an abstraction is much more difficult to deal with than "Mister Death," who is just a guy with a difficult job. In the same way, Heaven is a place, not merely another abstraction. Abstractions are the domain of wizened old philosophers, not kids with more energy than a barrel of monkeys.

When dealing with each other, children are straightforward, unencumbered by fear or embarrassment. With adults, they become even smaller than they really are. My task is to help them become Jack in the face of the giant, David in the face of Goliath, to confront problems and people with courage and directness. Again, they need not only encouragement to express their feelings and ideas but they need endorsement as well.

Once we have named and tamed the lion, we can teach him tricks. The best trick we can teach death is how wonderful life can be. The belief that life is wonderful has kept Mister Death in his corner for a long, long time.

J A K E

Jake was nine when we met. His prognosis was terminal, with an outside date of three months but, all things considered, three weeks might have been more realistic. He was hooked up to every machine except the coffeemaker. As I sat on his bed and watched him I wondered if he had ever been a healthy child. He hadn't.

Nothing was easy for Jake. Not eating, not breathing, not moving, and especially not talking. Talking took every bit of energy he had and left him gasping for air.

Mary, as usual, had some advice to offer.

"What am I supposed to do?" I whined, exasperated.

"Improvise, honey," she beamed at me. "You good at that."

"Yeah, right," I mumbled.

Jake was awake now and looked me over trying to figure me out.

"They call me Mister Silly," I volunteered. "I'm kinda the local nut, clown, goofball."

Jake frowned slightly and gave me what I took to be a quizzical look.

"OK, here's the deal. I come here and hang out with the kids and talk about what's on their minds. I'm not a doctor or a shrink or anything like that. I, er, make teddy bears and write stories. I'm sort of a go-between. You know, between the kids and the grownups."

I thought I saw him smile. I must admit that a six-foot-five, white-haired old man referring to "grownups" was a little bit funny.

In time, we found a way to communicate using finger signing, facial expressions, and grunting. Before too long we had a real dialogue going. I'd frame the conversation in questions like "How are you feeling today? Give me one finger for good and two fingers for not so hot." After a while we got pretty good at it and were talking up a storm.

Jake, like most of the kids, had a final wish. His was to have one more Christmas. Given his timetable, that seemed out of the question. I told him so and he let me know that he intended to stick it out. I told him that I believed in miracles, too.

As the days passed it became clear that he wasn't going to last until Christmas. What little hope I had that he might make it was discouraged by his doctors. His body just wasn't strong enough to last until December 25th.

When I told Jake this, he protested that he'd made a deal with God, and he knew that if he kept up his end of the bargain that surely God would honor His. I worried that my little buddy would lose his faith if God didn't come through. We talked and talked about how God answered prayers, and that sometimes his answer was "No." But Jake assured me that he'd make it.

I searched my mind and my heart for a solution. There were other factors adding to the problem. First, the battle to stay alive was stressing him, and actually harming him. Second, and more importantly, he wanted his family with him for Christmas, but they were hundreds of miles away. His father had been saving vacation and sick leave days just to be able to bring his family to see Jake before he died and to be with him at the end. But that meant only a few days. The problem here was timing.

For the next few days I talked to Jake about his condition and how there might be a way to get what he wanted—but he had to make a new bargain. If he got his wish for family and Christmas, he had to let go afterwards. He had to stop fighting death and accept the days, no matter how few, that life would give him. He agreed. I don't usually encourage bargaining of any kind, because it is usually unrealistic and just another way to avoid facing the reality of impending death. But this was different. Jake had faced the truth about death and he wasn't stalling for time, hoping for a cure. He just wanted another Christmas.

I told him to let me know when he thought it was time and together with his family, we'd make it Christmas, even though it was only September. His family was ready to come as soon as it was time, and all the Eggheads were busy making decorations and gifts for our early celebration. I got my Santa suit out of mothballs.

Three weeks later Jake lifted his index finger to let me know it was time.

On October 9th, Santa arrived with a bag of gifts and a chorus of bald reindeer singing "Jingle Bells." Surrounded by family and friends, Jake celebrated his last Christmas.

Later that night, Jake kept his end of the bargain— closed his eyes, and let go.

BARGAINING

In her definitive book, *On Death and Dying*, Elisabeth Kubler-Ross lists the stages a person facing death passes through. She points out that these stages often vary in order of appearance, and may overlap or be concurrent. They are: Denial, Isolation, Anger, Bargaining, Depression, and Acceptance. She also pays a great deal of attention to what she labels Hope, and the role it plays during all the stages.

I have certainly seen all of these elements at work in adults facing death, but I have seen fewer of them in children. Denial and Isolation in children usually take the form of Withdrawal and Confusion. The new hospital environment is a major contributing factor. The loss of parental protection is another—separation may contribute to their anger. Being stuck with needles by strangers in funny white coats is no picnic either, and can lead to depression.

But acceptance seems to come easier to children than adults. Their innocence seems to be the most obvious reason for this. They don't really understand death. And they trust adults. "If Mommy and Daddy say I'm going to die, then that's what I'm going to do."

Children spend a lot of time in the bargaining stage. They are born wheeler-dealers. While adults are busy playing "Let's Make A Deal" with God, children are negotiating with every adult they encounter. Being sick is bad enough, but being hospitalized is horrible, and they'll do anything to get out. They will promise anything to avoid staying in bed or taking a pill or getting stuck with a needle.

The deals are tempting: Perfect behavior. A clean room. The dishes every night. Homework. Babysit the baby. Walk the dog, and so on. If children do approach God, the deal usually involves their parents. If God lets them live they will (obey, love, fill in the blank) their parents.

There is a temptation to fall into a child's bargain trap, and a temptation to exploit it. Conning adults is not a talent, but a basic instinct. The old "I'll do _____ if you do _____," is a game kids are born knowing. But the reverse game can be played by the parents, and it can be dangerous.

"Take your medication and you'll get well," is a bargain adults may not be able to honor.

Doctors and nurses often slip into the trap of trying to encourage a child by bargaining over their therapy with promises of success. Bad bargain. And the kid is playing his own version of that game, too. "Will I get well if I let you stick that needle in my fanny?" Careful about that bargain, Doctor. You could end up a liar.

The one thing that children need to survive is trust. They must be able to trust adults. If you aren't careful, little Tommy's version of "Let's Make a Deal" could find you playing "Jeopardy" instead.

Bargaining for both the adult and the child facing death is merely a stall—a dash for the exit before Mister Death makes his entrance. A little bargaining is good for the soul; it helps us to clean up our acts. If we promise God to throw out the garbage in exchange for more time—more life—we may give up drugs or alcohol or unsafe sex or bad language or cigarettes or kicking the dog. But a little bargaining goes a long way, and should be cut short before it grows into a crutch or a fantasy. More than one terminal patient has told me that they made a deal with God and are going to live longer or be cured. I suggest to them that making promises in the dark is a dangerous thing. They might have just made a deal with the devil.

There are thousands of stories of people who have stayed alive long after their doctor's prediction. Sometimes they survive long enough to attend a wedding or see a grandchild born. Just as some people die for no apparent reason after their lifetime companion has gone, others survive with that same determination. The will to live and the will to die are very powerful, and the mind is a mighty force to be reckoned with.

A child's mind is fertile soil. So when we play "Let's Make a Deal" in Harmony, I try to get them to make good bargains.

Here are a few good deals that are always safe to bargain with.

I'll love you if you love me.

I'll tell the truth if you do.

I'll try to understand how you feel if you try to understand how I feel.

Let's trade hugs.

Let's trade secrets.

Let's trade fears.

But in the marketplace of death, there are no bargains, no deals. So there is only one deal, one prayer, that I encourage the children to make.

"If I have another day, I promise to live it the best I can."

M A R C I E

While Harmony seems to work for almost any age group, I find that very young children, those under seven, need more help in expressing themselves. In order to help them talk about their problems, I created two characters named Button and Blossom who faced similar problems and acted as surrogates for the children. As I told their stories the young ones would chime in and help or correct me, and in so doing, they revealed their own thoughts and feelings.

Button and Blossom helped in another way. They had great "attitude" about all that befell them and in this way they became role models for the younger kids to emulate. There are not many six-year-old heroes in the world today. Button and Blossom filled the void and met the challenge.

When Marcie entered the group she was almost seven years old. She was diagnosed with AIDS when she was six. Now she had Kaposi's Sarcoma, a cancer that reveals itself in purple patches on the skin. The patches start out small, but quickly enlarge to cover whole sections of the face and body. At first Marcie had only a few spots on her forehead, but they quickly enlarged to the area around her eyes.

Button and Blossom discovered a new friend one afternoon as the sun streamed across the floor and lit up Marcie's face.

Button and Blossom and the Magic Butterfly

Button had twisted his ankle, and Blossom had wrapped it with her pretty flowered scarf. He hopped along for a few steps and fell down again.

"I think we should rest awhile," said Blossom.

"It's getting dark and we have nowhere to stay the night," replied Button. "I think I can hop along if I make a crutch." He reached up and snapped a branch from a nearby tree.

"Hey!" cried a tiny voice, "quit shaking my house."

Button and Blossom looked around but couldn't see anyone.

"Who are you?" asked Blossom.

"Where are you?" asked Button.

"Up here in the tree," replied the tiny voice.

Then Button and Blossom saw a tiny, fuzzy caterpillar peeking out of its cocoon.

"Oh," said Blossom, "we're so sorry to have disturbed you, Sir."

"I'm not a sir, I'm a her," replied the caterpillar with fierce indignity. "And thank you very much."

"Oops, sorry," replied Blossom. "But it's hard to tell from just seeing your face just what you are."

"Well, I'm dressing at the moment and won't be out until tomorrow, but there's a soft spot behind the tree where you can sleep tonight. Tomorrow I'll show you my new outfit."

Button and Blossom curled up under the tree and fell into a deep sleep. When the sun awakened them they looked around for the caterpillar but found only an empty cocoon.

"I guess we overslept and missed her," said Blossom.

"No you didn't," said a voice. "I'm right here above your heads."

The children looked up, and saw a tiny butterfly dancing on the morning breeze. Her small wings were dotted with pale violet spots and she fluttered and glided around them, coming to rest on a low branch beside them.

"You were a brown caterpillar last night," remarked Button.

"Yes, but nature is magical, as you very well know, and now I'm a butterfly with lovely purple wings."

"You certainly are," replied Blossom. "I wish I had lovely violet wings and could fly too."

"You can," said the butterfly. "That's what magic is for."

Then the butterfly sat on each of their noses and shook some of her wing dust on their faces.

Button and Blossom looked at each other and saw that all around their eyes were lovely purple butterfly wing patterns.

They closed their eyes and flew through the air after the butterfly. It was a great adventure, and the three of them laughed and laughed all afternoon as they swooped and fluttered.

The next morning, the butterfly was gone, but they would always remember her.

When Marcie died, we had a special memorial service of our own for her. I painted their faces with purple butterfly wing designs and we danced in the park in her honor. She fluttered above us on wings of memory.

STORYTIME

Besides bringing bags of bears to the children, I brought stories. At first it was the usual stuff, fairy tales, comic books, and even stuff from *National Geographic*. If you're stuck in a hospital room all day, your fantasy life exists beyond those pale walls.

After a while, I began making up stories, and later I got the kids to join in and make up their own adventures. Since I had no formal training for all this, I kind of made it up as I went along. After trial and error, I finally developed a formula for storytime. Here's how it works.

We all sit in a circle, and I ask one person to pick a hero and another to pick a villain. Then I ask another kid to pick the place and another to pick the problem. Then, we need one good thing that happens and one bad thing. OK, let's tell a story.

"Mark, pick a hero."

"A spotted puppy."

"Susan, you pick a villain."

"The Dogcatcher."

"OK, Bobby, what's the problem?"

"The puppy wants to free his friends who got caught by the Dogcatcher."

"Emily, what's the bad thing."

"It's very dark outside."

"Nick, what's the good thing."

"The puppy has a magic firefly friend."

"Well, let's see, we have . . ."

"Bear!"

"Yes, Vicky."

"You didn't pick the place. May I please pick the place?"

"OK." I reply.

"A big, dark forest beyond the city," she replies earnestly.

And so we begin the story, with all the kids helping to develop the plot line as we go along.

Somewhere in the course of telling these stories the kids reveal their hopes and dreams as well as their deepest fears. Is Vicky's "dark forest beyond the city" her imagined place of death? Is Mark's spotted puppy a version of himself? And is the

Dogcatcher really Mister Death in a new disguise? Sometimes yes, and other times no. With kids not everything has a hidden meaning.

For years we have been following the adventures of Button and Blossom who are trying to escape the King of Darkness and find the Kingdom of Light. It is our version of a soap opera that goes on and on, and on, shaped by their needs and desires.

These groups of terminally ill children constantly change in number for a variety of reasons. One child may be in the hospital for a series of treatments and may then go back home. Others go into remission and go home. Others die. As each child enters and leaves the group the story line changes to include them in some way.

When Emily died a few months later, the children wanted to tell a story about her. She was, of course, the heroine, and Mister Death was the villain.

"What is the bad thing that happens?" I asked.

"That she got sick and died," replied Nick.

"And what's the good thing, Vicky?"

"That we all loved her."

I think that these stories are like sunshine. They illuminate, comfort, warm, and heal.

S H A R O N

We were sitting in Harmony when it occurred to me that we hadn't been in anyone's face for quite a while, and I thought it was time to stir things up. We settled on a "bald" theme, and we discussed several possible celebrations of bald living. Easter was coming but we'd all tired of the pink bunny, painted Egghead routine. We discussed Easter bonnets but that was deemed politically incorrect given our bald agenda.

"How about an Egghead Miss America Pageant?" I suggested.

Howls of laughter applauded my suggestion.

"We could decorate our heads the way hairy kids can't." suggested Wendy.

"We can be the contestant's escorts," added Billy.

"Yeah, we can wear those fancy black suits." Tommy chimed in.

"What could we do to our heads that no one else can?" asked Roberta.

"Well," I suggested. "You could stencil designs on them or paste flowers and bows to them—even fake jewels."

"Wow," responded Wendy. "That's cool."

"Can the guys fake-tattoo their heads too?" asked Tommy.

"Anything you guys want." I replied. "And I'll be the host and sing, "Here she comes, Miss Egghead America . . .""

They screamed with laughter.

"Oh, god, Mister Silly—don't sing," cried Sharon.

"Yeah, man, you have a terrible voice," howled Robert.

"But politically correct," offered Wendy. "Very in-your-face."

"Yeah, right," laughed Robert. "OK, Mister S, you can sing—a little."

"Thanks, guys."

So the plans were made, and the date was set, and the invitations were sent. It was a great in-your-face event. There they were, in all their baldness, strutting to the music and changing the way we see things.

The boys were the escorts and the judges. I played Bert Parks, and sang a little. The girls had secretly prepared their "head-dresses," and so each one was a total surprise to the boys. They helped each other get ready, and I pitched in with paint and paste to make things work.

Hospital staff and families were invited, and one after another, the girls strutted their stuff down the runway. Heads were covered in jewels and flowers, and African designs, and moss, with a butterfly bouncing overhead. There were brightly colored bows and tiny reflecting mirrors like a ballroom dome.

And then there were the boys, in the tuxedos that I hustled from a good-natured shop owner, with tattoos proclaiming that they, too, could be pretty. The theme, of course, was "Bald is Beautiful."

Milk and cookies were served while the camcorders whirled, capturing every moment.

The votes were tallied, and Sharon was crowned Miss Egghead America. In the talent portion she had sung "I Feel Pretty" from the musical, *West Side Story*.

Pretty is as pretty does.

P R E T T Y

Recently Oprah did a show on death and dying. There were lots of PWAs (People With AIDS) in the audience, and at one point, a handsome young gay man stood up and said that he would commit suicide if the effects of AIDS disfigured him. "I like being pretty," he said. "I couldn't live in an ugly body. I'd rather die first."

Oprah recalled that one of her coworkers also liked being pretty and had died of AIDS. The man then admitted that he'd already had a serious bout with Kaposi's Sarcoma, had been covered with the purple blotches the cancer causes, and he hadn't killed himself. He'd gotten well again, and at the moment he was feeling fit as a fiddle and looking pretty as a picture.

I'm sure that members of the audience as well as millions of viewers at home might have thought his attitude was shallow, even silly. Only a fool would kill himself over not being pretty anymore. Yeah, right!

That's why middle-aged people fill America's gyms and Weight Watchers is a billion-dollar enterprise with a host of imitators. It's why Clairol sells millions in youthful hair color products and wrinkle creams earn millions from dissatisfied customers.

Ponce de Leon wasn't the only fool looking for the fountain of youth. Too many of us equate who we are with how we look—to ourselves and to others. So I'm not surprised that Oprah's guest might want to check out before things got ugly.

Pretty is as pretty does, the saying goes. I'm not sure if that means that having a pretty spirit gives you a pretty face, or what. But if that *is* the meaning of pretty, then every dying child I have met is a real beauty. The knowledge of death enriches the spirit of life. It may take time, it may be a struggle, but sooner or later the dying discover the beauty of being alive, one pretty day at a time. It's a lesson we all need to learn, because like it or not, we all have a ticket out of here. The dying just have a timetable.

But being a little princess and losing your long golden curls to chemotherapy is not the way the fairy tale goes. No self-respecting frog prince wants to be kissed by a fuzztop Egghead.

It is vital for sick children to feel good about themselves and not be saddled with a lack of self-esteem. That's the lesson the Eggheads learned when I taught them to stand tall and toss their caps away.

Bald *is* beautiful!

B O B B Y

Mid-May, and the promise of summer was everywhere. Birds chirped and buds popped out along slim branches. Rebirth and renewal. Life, pouring its sap of rejuvenation into every living thing.

T-shirt weather. I was assaulted by hundreds of brightly colored shirts with gaudy proclamations. Everything from "Hard Rock Cafe," to "Go Jets," to "Yabba Dabba Doo!"

Somewhere, in my dim memory, I recall something Fran Lebowitz, the delightful New York writer and premier grump, once penned on the subject of T-shirts with messages. It was something to the effect, "If people don't listen to you, what makes you think they want to hear from your underwear?"

Good point—*unless* you want to get in their face!

Good old grumpy Franny got me to thinking about the kids, and what they had to say about their situation and feelings. Maybe someone *would* listen to their underwear. So I encouraged them to make their own outspoken T-shirts. We call it "getting-it-off-my-chest-and-onto-my-chest" therapy.

Children faced with death offer simple, crystal-clear visions of innocent acceptance. Old people, shaped by a lifetime of dreams and prayers answered and unanswered cling to life with a fierceness that challenges us to be better at living.

I've used this T-shirt therapy with both young and old. These are some of the messages they have sent out to the world around them.

DON'T EMPOWER DEATH
Susan, age 10, cancer

LOOKING FOR A BLESSING
Jenny, age 12, leukemia

CHECK YOUR TIMETABLE
Rose, age 57, old age

NEVER TOO LATE
Thomas, age 90, cancer

HUG ME——I'M HUMAN
Stephen, age 22, AIDS

IT'S YOUR PROBLEM——KEEP IT!
Robert, age 16, AIDS

PLEASE DON'T FEED MY FEARS
Sylvia, age 47, cancer

LIFE IS A TERMINAL CONDITION
Richard, age 23, AIDS

WE ARE ALL TERMINAL——ENJOY TODAY
Barbara, age 32, AIDS

But all the T-shirts that I have seen and helped to make, the one that stays with me most vividly is the one made by an eight-year-old named Bobby, who believed in reincarnation:

NEXT TIME A RAINBOW

P R O T E S T

> *Rage, rage against the dying of the light,*
> *do not go gentle into that good night.*

These words of protest, penned by the poet Dylan Thomas, show the power of words in the face of death.

Words are often the illumination in the darkness of fear. If we speak the words of our fear or anger aloud, their power over us is diminished. I like to say "A lion named is a lion tamed." Somehow, if I call a lion "Chuckles," he is less threatening. Instead of a man-eating beast of the jungle he seems like a charming cartoon character.

Working with children who face death is as complex as travelling through a maze blindfolded. You must grope your way, one step at a time, hitting dead-ends and backtracking to begin again. Often, what works one day fails the next. There are no easy one-two punches that are always effective.

Being Mister Silly allows me to take liberties that the more serious doctors and therapists cannot. So I use my role of court jester to reduce the dreaded lion to a cartoon character.

While we discuss death seriously from time to time, I try to keep death from becoming too heavy to handle. By simply referring to death as "Mister Death" I take him out of the shadows and into the light. Look, he's just a little Charlie Chaplin character with a difficult job.

I try to get the kids to claim their feelings. Children want to please, and they take blame too readily. We all know stories of children who feel responsible when their parents divorce. We have seen children cry that they'll "be good" if only Daddy won't move away. They can't see their parents' failure and weakness—only their own.

In the same way, children who are very sick know the hardship it places on their families, and they feel responsible. Children, as innocent as they are, do not understand the concept of being a victim. So they take too much blame for things, and they try too hard to please.

When I first started working with the Eggheads, they all wore caps. I quickly discovered that it was for the benefit of staff and family, who they sensed were uncomfortable in their balding presence. I taught them to use their baldness as a badge of courage. Chemotherapy was their weapon, and they were fighting their enemy of disease. Their baldness was the result of their battle, and like wounded heroes, they should be proud (not ashamed) of it.

I was working a fund-raising auction for a children's hospital, and had brought one of my Egghead buddies to tug at the heartstrings—and hopefully at the purse strings—of those who came.

We sat up on the dais, looking out at the healthy and wealthy who had paid a hundred bucks for chicken à la king and melting ice cream. Speeches were made. Jack was introduced, and he made a little speech about how much he appreciated their help. He wore a red baseball cap to cover his baldness but it peeked out behind his ears.

My job was to hustle the audience into buying beautifully made teddy bears, which had been donated by artists all across the country. These are handmade Teddys that bring hundreds, even thousands, of dollars in retail.

Jumping into my best Mister Silly persona, I teased the audience by saying they couldn't bid less than their age or waist size. I offered a bonus of a big bear hug and a kiss on the cheek if they'd up their bids another hundred.

But this night I had an ace up my sleeve. As the bidding began I had Jack stand up and take off his cap. The overhead lights glistened off his hairless dome. The room got very quiet, and I announced that tonight we were not only going to put a smile on this little boy's face but on his bald head as well. Jack tilted his head towards me and I drew two eyes and a tiny mouth on the very top. Then he faced the audience and I announced that for every thousand dollars we raised I'd increase the smile on his head. As the evening progressed, Jack's smile got bigger and bigger and bigger until he had a fifteen-thousand-dollar happy face drawn on the top of his gleaming dome.

Who says a picture's only worth a thousand words!

B i l l y

We walked along the beach, stooping to pick up shells, beach glass, and bits of driftwood for one of Billy's projects. At 16, Billy looked like a typical teenager, with a mop of sun-streaked hair and patch or two of acne. He came to Harmony a month ago after he learned that he was HIV-positive. I didn't ask him how he thought he became infected. It didn't matter.

At first he just sat in Harmony in silence, soaking up the words of the others who faced an even more immediate death.

"You aren't sore at me for not taking part in the sessions are you, Ted?" he asked.

"No, of course not. That's your choice—but I wonder why you ask. Looking for a little rejection, or maybe a kick in the butt, to get you off square one?"

"Who knows?" he answered, bending down to pick up a shell. "I'm having a difficult time trying to figure out what to say. Those little kids seem so much smarter than me."

"They've had a lot longer to deal with the idea of death than you have—and they still have that edge of innocence. You're on the edge of being an adult. You are beginning to see dying the way adults do."

"How's that?"

"Being shortchanged at the booth on the highway of life."

"Yeah, I guess so. I mean, I guess that is what I think about. All the stuff I won't get to do."

"Bzzzzzz, WRONG answer!" I replied.

"Why?"

"Well, for starters, you don't know when you'll die. You might not die at all if they find a cure in your lifetime. Besides, if you give up now you miss all the fun of the moment. And think what a jerk you'll feel like if that happens," I answered.

"Yeah, yeah, I know all that stuff but I haven't bought into it yet. I'm still feeling down, ya know."

"That's OK, as long as you see it for what it is."

"What's that?"

"Stalling for time."

"Huh?"

"As long as you stay in this space you don't have to move ahead to the next one. Widows do it all the time. They stay in their widow space because it's nice and cozy and everyone lets them. It's a victim space. A 'poor me' space. If they move forward they have to become responsible for their life again, for what they do and what happens to them. That's not easy. In fact, it's pretty tough. So they stay where they are. It's what they know and it's safe."

We walked in silence for a while, picking up debris and an occasional bit of wonder.

"I know you're right, but I just can't get a hold on it. I'm still doing 'Why me?' and it's my fault. I have to work my way through that first."

"Jump over it. It's doggy-do."

"What?"

"Jump over it because it's doggy-do—if you don't step or jump over it, then you'll step in it and get it on your feet."

"What does that mean?"

"Seems clear to me. What is doggy-do? It's waste. It's processed Puppy Chow and it stinks."

"Yeah?"

"Asking 'Why me?' and thinking it's your fault is a waste too. And it stinks. Why NOT you? Life's a lottery. Win or lose, you're in the game. Taking blame is not the same thing as taking responsibility. Responsibility is locking the barn BEFORE the horse is stolen. After that everything is a waste of time. Spilt milk. Mop it up and move on. If there is a lesson then learn it—but that's the end of it."

"But I don't know what to do, Ted."

"LIVE. It is just that simple. You are still healthy, still able to be here on this beach. Still able to pick up shells. So, do it. And when the time comes, you'll die just the same as everyone else."

"I'm going to get AIDS."

"That's just the name of your disease. It isn't you. It isn't what you are or who you are. You are Billy. Period. And you are HIV-positive and you have acne and blonde hair and a doggy-do point of view."

"Screw you, Mister Silly." He laughed, kicking sand all over me. "OK, I'll try to move on. I'll try to get off this square."

The next week during our Harmony session he spoke up for the first time.

"Ted kicked my butt last week and I really tried to move ahead, tried to get off the dime, but I just kept lingering there. I couldn't see beyond the moment, and I felt lousy about everything. I'm sittin' around listening to creeps on talk shows and these wise guys with answers, and I'm thinking, *what a bunch of jerks.* Everyone yelling, nobody listens, and the host stands there cracking up over the stupidity of it all. I'm eating cake and drinking coke and playing with the shells we picked up at the beach and I hear some guy say something like, 'The better you feel about yourself the better the world around you looks' and it hit me. That's taking responsibility.

"So I thought I'd come here and tell you that I'm off square one and movin' on. I've got days I want to live and that's what I'm going to do."

Getting off square one is one of the toughest things we have to do in life. Whether it's looking for a new job, or starting a diet or facing the end of your life, sometimes we need a little assistance. Perhaps a gentle nudge or maybe a good swift kick in the pants.

Like the man says, "Ya have to keep on keepin' on."

T E A R S

Recently I heard a report on the chemistry of tears. It said that the chemical content of tears varies from tears of joy and tears of sorrow.

Now, I am a great champion of tears. I love to cry when I'm sad *and* when I'm happy. I'm one of those men for whom tears are not a problem, and I thank my lucky stars for that.

Sitting across from one of my teddy-bear buddies in a coffee shop around the corner from the hospital we had just visited, I noticed that she was on the verge of tears.

"Barbara, what's the matter?"

"Oh, God, it's just so sad. I don't know how you do it week after week. How can you face them knowing they are so close to death. It tears me up just thinking about it."

"Are you afraid to die, Barbara?" I asked gently.

"Of course I am. Everyone is."

"I'm not."

"What? You can't be serious. Do you mean to say that way down deep you aren't scared of dying?"

"I'm uneasy about not knowing what death is, but I'm not afraid of it."

"I don't believe you, Ted. I think that basically everyone is scared to death of dying."

I laughed. Barbara frowned.

"Listen to what you just said. You said that everyone is 'scared to death of dying' and I think that's amusing. Don't you?"

"No, I don't."

"Well, you should. Being frightened of the unknown is one thing, but being frightened of something as well known as death is foolish. Sooner or later we've all got to do it. Our species has been doing it since day one. But in a way there is a germ of truth in your remark. I think everyone is afraid of the process of dying. Yes, I'm afraid of dying, but not of death."

"Isn't it the same thing, after all?" replied Barbara.

"No, I don't think so. I think that there is a great difference between the two. In some ways, it's a matter of faith. Not faith in a religious sense but faith in the process. Are you afraid of flying?"

"No."

"Why not? Thousands of rational people are."

"Well, I'm not."

"OK, you're afraid of dying but not of flying. Maybe you accept the premise of flying better than the premise of dying. But do you know enough about flight to really accept that premise and be secure with it? My guess is that you really aren't secure, but you have faith in the process because you have seen it work more often than not. So without a moment's hesitation you climb on board a plane and fly away.

"Now think about this. Planes fly perfectly most of the time—maybe 95% of the time, and so you feel secure with that process. Dying works 100% of the time, but you're not secure in that process. Think about that."

"That's just babble, Ted."

"No, Barbara, it isn't. It is simply fact. Not every plane takes off and lands perfectly, but every living thing dies perfectly. It is the one thing we do in life perfectly. No miss, no error."

Barbara stared at her coffee a moment and then looked up at me.

"I'm still afraid of dying, no matter what you say."

"I believe you are. I believe most people are. But life has taught me not to be. And those kids have taught me not to be. They have taught me to be fearless—to be courageous in the face of death."

"They're innocent and don't know any better."

"Exactly. And we should learn from them and reclaim our innocence and our faith in the process."

"I still want to cry for them."

"Tears of joy for their life. Tears of joy for their daily triumphs. But no tears of sorrow for what will never be. Not every candle has a long wick, but it still gives light and warmth."

"But they—we—will never know what they might have been, what they might have done if they had lived."

"Barbara, do you know who Ryan White was?"

"Sure. The little boy who died of AIDS."

"Tell me this, Barbara, if you can. Do you think Ryan White could have touched more lives or influenced more people if he had lived to be a hundred years old? I think that children are messengers who bring us the truth we have lost sight of as we grow older. Hundreds of adults died of AIDS, but no one really listened until a child spoke to them. Then they stopped to listen. It's not an answer, Barbara, but it is a point of view."

"It still breaks my heart thinking about them and I'm still afraid of dying. You can't convince me."

"Well," I smiled and touched her hand. "I can't win them all."

As I headed back home alone I remembered an afternoon in August more than ten years ago. I had been working with my first group of terminal children and had grown to love them all. One afternoon I went to visit them and learned that little Lisa, age six, had died the night before. I got through the afternoon without crying. I listened to the others talk about her and about her death and how they felt about it. As I closed the door behind me and started down the hall towards the elevators, it hit me square in the chest like a heart attack. I began to tremble and my knees felt like rubber. I ducked into a stairwell and sat on the top step, my hands clutching the iron shafts of the handrail, and sobbed uncontrollably. Wave after wave of tears racked my body until there were no tears left. Then I went home.

I thought that I was crying for Lisa, but I was really crying for myself—for my loss. Later, when I remembered her laughter, her sheer delight with life, and her determination to get the answers to all her questions, I cried again for her and the gifts she had given me.

L A U R I E

Laurie and I were sitting together braiding daisies into a garland for her hair. I had hoped to be able to take her outside today, but the spring rain washed away that plan. Instead, I brought her a bouquet of daisies, and some pink ribbon to make a Victorian halo.

"This would be a lot prettier if I still had long hair instead of this fuzz."

"Well," I replied, "your fuzz is quite pretty, little princess. It looks just like spring grass." And just like the new spring grass, the fuzz on Laurie's head indicated rebirth—she had completed her chemo series and was on her way to remission and possible recovery.

"Is my daddy coming today?" she asked.

"No, but your mommy is." How, I wondered, do you tell a child who has beaten death at his own game that her daddy did not? Felled by a heart attack in his sleep.

"Did my daddy go away?"

"Yes, how did you know that?" I asked, puzzled.

"I felt it. When he came and kissed me the other night I knew he was going away."

"When did that happen?"

"Two nights ago. He visited me and kissed me while I was sleeping. Can I wear it now? Is it finished?"

I put the garland on her head and watched as she gazed in her little hand mirror.

"Am I pretty now, Bear?"

"Very pretty, princess." I replied truthfully. She rewarded my honesty and good taste with a gleeful hug.

"I'm pretty." She giggled as she danced around the room. At six and three quarters, almost seven, she was a beautiful little child, wide-eyed and innocent. She was a strong fighter and had beaten the odds and survived. She told me once that she had given Mister Death a kick in the behind, an expression she had heard an older boy use when he went into remission.

I wondered about her dream about her father. This was not the first time I had heard of people appearing in dreams at their moment of death.

"Laurie," I asked. "Did your daddy say anything before he kissed you the other night?"

"No, he just smiled and kissed me but I knew he loved me anyway."

"Laurie, when your mommy comes, I want you to tell her about Daddy first thing. Promise?"

"Sure." She danced off, twirling to the music in her head. "Let's do a daisy for Daddy." She picked up a daisy and plucked off the petals, chanting "loves me, loves me not" until the last petal remained. "LOVES ME!" she chirped with delight, and returned to her dance. I looked up and saw her mother standing in the doorway. She was the color and shape of a recent widow.

"MOMMY!" cried Laurie as she caught sight of her mother. "Aren't I pretty? Bear, says I am. We made a 'torian garland from daisies, and Daddy loves me—the daisy says so." She hugged her mother and led her towards me. Her mother's eyes were filled with tears and I hoped that she could hang on long enough to hear Laurie's dream.

"Laurie," I said softly. "What did you want to tell Mommy?"

"Oh, yes," she smoothed her dress as if preparing for a recital and faced her mother who was sitting next to me. "Daddy visited me the other night and kissed me while I was sleeping and when I woke up I knew he was going away. He went away didn't he? Bear says he did."

"Oh, baby," cried her mother as she pulled her into her arms. "Mommy and Daddy love you. We will always love you."

We sat and explained to Laurie about her daddy. She listened carefully but didn't say anything. Her mother cried, and she cried, and kept saying, "Don't cry Mommy," the way children always do when they see their parents cry.

Several weeks later, in a Harmony session, Laurie offered us this observation about her father's death.

"My daddy went to heaven to make sure everything will be OK when I get there."

I knew she was right.

F A C E S

In the world of the dying there are many faces—and a few too many masks.

One afternoon as we sat in a circle, breathing our way to Harmony, the subject of faces came up.

"I hate the faces that the doctors and nurses put on," said Karen, who is ten. "They're so phony with their nice smiles and soft voices. That little smile before they jab another needle in your ass."

"Fanny. You're not supposed to say ass," chided Betty, who is seven. "It isn't nice."

"Yeah, well a needle in your fanny isn't nice and neither is a phony smile."

Everyone agreed.

"I hate the face my parents make when they come to visit," said Seth. "I wish just once they would look the way they feel. You know, scared and sad."

"Or angry," remarked Karen. "I wish just once they'd look as angry as I know they feel. At least my sister is honest enough to say how she feels."

"How does she feel?" I asked.

"Mad as hell, that's how! And her face shows it. She's mad because my sickness screws up her life too. Everything at home revolves around my sickness. When they consider doing anything it depends on how I am doing. She had to give up her ballet classes because my parents can't take her there on weekends—because they have to come here to see me. It isn't fair to her and it isn't fair to me."

"How is it unfair to you?" I asked.

"I just want to be like her—just another child in the family—not the center of everything like I am now. Pretty soon she'll start to hate me."

"My brother hates me," said Lonny softly. "He says I spoiled his life by getting sick. He says it's my fault that he isn't going to camp this summer because my medicine costs so much. He says he wishes I was dead already. He's really mad at me for getting sick. I told him it wasn't my fault, but he doesn't care."

"Wow. How does that make you feel?" asked Karen.

"At least he's honest about it," replied Lonny. "At least he doesn't give me THE FACE."

THE FACE isn't a face at all, but rather, a mask. I have watched the parents mold their faces into little smiles of courage and encouragement hundreds of times—frozen expressions with haunted, often terrified, eyes looking out. Painted on expressions that hide the truth, the fear and the dread.

And the children, desperate to please their parents, mirror these expressions and join in the game of deception. And when the parents leave, their shoulders drop as if the wind has been knocked out of them. They struggle to put one foot in front of the other as they move unsteadily towards the hospital exit and back into the world of the living.

Meanwhile, back in the world of the dying, the children's faces ache from smiling, and they relax a moment before picking up their stuff and going back to their rooms.

"Mister Silly, do we make you sad?" asks Lonny.

"Yes, sometimes," I reply.

"Do you ever cry?"

"Yes."

"Thank you, Mister Silly." My honesty earns me a tight hug.

The circle is very quiet today. Everyone is looking forward to the weekend and another round of visits from their families. Another visit from THE FACE.

"I wish just once my father would cry or even look sad," says Karen. "I wish my mother would stop dressing up and wearing makeup. I want to see her messy in an apron they way she looks in our kitchen back home."

"I wish my daddy didn't wear a tie when he comes here. I wish he'd wear his sweatshirt and baseball cap," said Tommy.

"I wish just once they'd call up and say that they couldn't come because they had to take my sister somewhere. I'd miss them but I wouldn't have to feel guilty and I wouldn't have to look at their faces," said Karen.

"Hey, you guys are getting me down," I remarked. "You're acting like there's nothing you can do to change this. Come on, let's make a plan."

"What kind of plan, Mister Silly?"

"OK, let's find a way to let your parents know that you don't like THE FACE and you don't like the pretending."

"How can we do that?" asked Lonny.

"Be creative. Think of something. What is it about THE FACE that bothers you most?"

"It isn't real. It's phony," said Karen.

"So it's a mask," I suggested.

"Exactly," replied Karen.

"So . . ." I hinted, ". . . it's a MASK!"

"We could wear masks too," suggested Betty.

And so that weekend, when their parents arrived, the children were all sitting in a row wearing silly masks with big smiles drawn on them. It was hard to tell one child from another and the parents, caught off guard, dropped their pretense for a moment. The children spoke.

"My name is Karen. I have cancer. I am going to die. Can you see how I feel behind this mask?"

"My name is Lonny. I have cancer. I am going to die. Can you see how I feel behind this mask?"

"My name is Betty. I am HIV-positive. Can you see how I feel behind this mask?"

"My name is Robert, and I will take off my mask and show you how I feel—if you will take off yours and show me how you feel."

B E L I N D A

A few months after my first book was published, I was invited
to do a television show about how children felt about death
and dying. While almost all my experience was with critical and
terminally ill children, the guests on this show were supposed
to be a cross-section of "well" children.

When I arrived at the TV studio, the children (about 25
of them) were assembled on a small set of bleachers. They
ranged in age from about seven to twelve, and were a
mix of boys and girls from various ethnic and socio-
economic backgrounds.

We had about forty-five minutes till air time, and I was
supposed to "warm them up" so that by the time the show
started we'd be comfortable together. They were a delightful,
well-behaved group, and I was impressed by their openness.
I introduced them to my teddy bear, Hug, and told them how
I had earned the name of Mister Silly. We laughed together,
and after a few minutes they were smiling and asking questions
just like any other group of kids I've worked with.

Towards the end of the warm-up, a pretty girl of nine leaned forward and whispered to me.

"Mister Silly, may I tell you a secret?" she asked.

"Of course, Belinda," I replied as a scanned her nametag.

"I'm dying."

Just like that. I was dumbfounded by her directness.

"It's a secret," she continued. "My parents don't want anyone to know because they want my life to be as normal as possible. These are my two best friends (indicating the girls sitting on either side of her) and we came here today to meet you because they aren't handling it too well."

I smiled at her two friends. Their bewilderment at her openness about her impending death was written clearly on their faces. I have seen that expression a hundred times before.

"Maybe you could help them understand what's happening to me," Belinda said quietly, "and that it's OK for them to be sad. I *want* them to be sad."

"How are *you* doing?" I asked looking into her brown eyes.

"Oh, I'm fine. I understand everything. I'm just worried about them."

During the taping, I got her friends to open up and talk about their feelings on their approaching loss, and their love and concern for their friend. She sat there beaming, as if she were opening gifts on her birthday. And she was—gifts of fear and concern and love and loss. Gifts she needed, to prepare for her last goodbye.

While I was talking to her parents I noticed the three of them giggling together and I wondered what the merriment was all about. I joined them and asked what was going on.

"We think that boy in the red jacket is soooo cute," replied Belinda with a smile.

S E C R E T S

All terminally ill children I've met have to deal with two subtle side effects of their illnesses: their parent's secrecy, and their concern for those they're leaving behind.

With the possible exception of AIDS, most terminal patients do not have a need for secrecy. But concerned parents do—they want to spare their child the added pressure such openness may bring.

The parents want to be "normal" for as long as possible. Children can be extremely cruel to those they think are weaker. So loving, concerned parents cloak their child's condition in deception, and call it protection.

I wonder at times who they are really protecting. Children need to tell the truth, and they need to hear it. It is terrible enough to learn that there is a killer inside your body without the added burden of shame and secrecy. No matter how we handle the situation, the truth usually is better than a lie. I'm not suggesting that the parents make a general proclamation to the neighbors, but I think it is important that key friends and teachers know about the situation. All terminally ill people need a support system to keep their courage and determination up.

In addition, children facing death often turn their concern outwards, to others. Almost from the beginning they are worried about everything from their parents and siblings to their puppies and collections of baseball cards. For that reason, I have them draw up a will. It empowers them. It allows them to take control of their lives while they still can. A child—even more than an adult—will put loved ones ahead of himself.

Over and over I hear in their questions and remarks, "What will happen to (fill in the blank) after I die?" I have heard many an eighty-year-old say that no one will miss them, but I have never heard those words from an eight-year-old.

There are many theories about how children develop, and why they behave as they do. Some say that infants are totally self-absorbed and think that their every whim and need is the center of the universe. Usually it is, to the parents. Then the child grows and learns to share the world with others. They begin to grasp subtleties in responses of parents and friends. A child sees and feels that he can make others happy and angry and sad.

Even more importantly, they accept responsibility for creating those responses. So terminally ill children are very concerned that what they are about to do—die—will have a horrible effect on those whom they love and who love them. In many ways, children still think that they are the centers of their universe. Possibly they feel that way until puberty. Perhaps we all feel that way until we die.

One of the most difficult and, at the same time, most loving gifts a parent or loved one can give a child facing death is to reassure them that everything will be OK after they are gone. Accomplishing this is about as easy as walking a tightrope over the Grand Canyon blindfolded with a severe case of hiccups.

But, it is essential. Any bitter pill, wrapped in unconditional love, can be swallowed.

Every terminal child, sooner or later, asks "I'm OK, but are you OK?" They need to know the answer—whatever it is.

M A R Y A N N

Maryann has orange hair and huge brown eyes. At ten she is like a porcelain doll, exquisite and fragile. Her normally ivory skin is paled by her illness, leukemia. There was a time when this disease was almost always fatal, especially in children. Today, things are better for most—but not for everyone. Maryann is not among the lucky ones who have rejoined the healthy and the living. Maryann is still fighting for her life. And what a lovely warrior she is.

She is the perfect example of grace under pressure.

"Did your ever read *Jane Eyre*?" she asks.

"Yes, and I saw the movie too," I reply. "Have you seen the movie?"

"Many times. It's a favorite of mine. Wasn't Elizabeth Taylor amazing in that movie? She was so beautiful."

"Yes, she was. But I think the little niece, Margaret O'Brien, was even more tragic."

"Maybe, but she didn't die."

"She didn't have much of a life either," I responded.

"All those old novels make death so romantic. Everyone dies so beautifully. Like Beth in *Little Women*. I don't think that's how it really is." She looks for my response.

"Candy-coated bitter pills."

"Yes." She looks away. "Too bad you can't do that in real life."

"Something bothering you today?"

"My medication and therapy aren't working. We're running out of options. I'm thinking about where I want to die and when."

"What are you saying, really?"

"Well, I'm not talking suicide, if that crossed your mind. I'm talking about taking over my life and making some decisions. I don't want a trip to Disneyland before I die, or to go to Europe, or to meet a movie star. I think I want to be in the country in a cottage, and just live the rest of my life without thinking about being sick and dying. I want to live my life and die as if I didn't know what was coming."

"What's stopping you?"

"What *isn't* stopping me. Family. Doctors. Everyone and every-thing. They're all so dedicated to keeping me alive that they can't see I have no life. You know, most of us feel that way from time to time, but right now I'm feeling it a lot more than usual. I've started to think about what I'm going to miss. I'll never fall in love. Never marry and have children. Never go to work.

Never grow old with my grandchildren. I hate that. I hate feeling and thinking that. It's bad for me. Bad for the life I have.

"I've been reading about people who stopped trying to 'stay alive' and went out and started living. We've talked about this a lot, but now I'm really thinking that that might be the direction I should take. What do you think?"

What I thought about was the last fiery dance of the autumn leaves and what a beautiful process of death it was. Maybe Maryann felt the same way. Maybe she wanted life to be more romantic as death approached, the way it was in a Victorian novel. Maybe she wanted to be in a field of flowers, and not in a room with pale green walls and blinking machines.

Maybe the leaves have the right idea.

L I V I N G

"There is really only one decision you have to make. Either you spend whatever time you have *staying* alive or you spend that time *being* alive."

This is my quiet friend Ed speaking to an auditorium filled with PWAs. Like him, they are dying. Like him, they are wondering about staying and being alive.

"I read stories about how Steve McQueen raced around the world looking for a cure for his cancer. I think it's a waste of time. I have friends trying to smuggle drugs from Paris into this country and I think it's a waste of time. And I don't want to waste my time!"

This is my quiet friend Ed pounding the lectern like a hellfire and brimstone preacher, and I think of the words, "With the knowledge of death comes the meaning of life."

Ed, who never knew when it was his turn to speak, and thus became a listener, was now speaking out loud and clear. "Don't give up your life trying to stay alive!" Shouting now, arms outstretched, "I CLAIM MY LIFE!"

I think of the kids rushing out to greet the day, knowing it could be their last, and I almost envy them. I envy their agenda—their timetable. They embrace the simple knowledge of being alive for another wonderful, wonder-filled day. And I long to have their zeal for being alive.

When I first came to the hospital, Mary put me to work rocking babies. I'd sit in a big wooden rocking chair and hold them against my chest so they could hear my heart beat and I'd watch them sleep. Sometimes they'd clutch my finger with a strength I couldn't imagine in such a tiny grasp. They had a hold on life that amazed me. And if they were sick I watched them fight to stay alive—screaming to drive the demons away.

And when they woke up and looked up at me I searched their eyes to see what lay beyond in all that innocence. And if they smiled. . . .

I have watched toddlers, pushing themselves along in bright-colored walkers, dragging their IV tubes behind them. Nothing stops them in their passionate quest for life.

And in the circles of Harmony, I hear them talk of death and life and how to deal with what is happening to them. And in their own voice and in their own way they say what my quiet friend Ed said:

"I CLAIM MY LIFE!"

S E T H

Children and old people have a great deal in common, not the least of which is their feisty attitude. There are sweet old grannies that will give you a piece of their mind at the drop of a hat—often in language strong enough to make a truck driver blush. I'm talking about having guts and gusto.

I heard about an experiment where orphans were brought to visit an old folks home, so I thought it might be interesting to see what would happen if I brought some terminally ill kids to meet some terminally ill old folks. What, I wondered, would these children with such short lives have to teach these old cronies who'd lived so long? And vice versa.

It was warm enough to take our little group outside for a picnic, so Mary and I gathered them up and set out on the grand adventure. There we were, a merry band of children and seniors in walkers and wheelchairs, getting ready to take on Mister Death. I wished my grandmother could have been a part of this group. She had so much natural wisdom and she was so filled with life that I was sure she'd have this group up and dancing in no time. I invoked her spirit to join us, and hoped she wasn't too busy elsewhere to respond.

We found a grassy knoll and settled down to talk. I figured that I'd start off and set the tone.

"I'd like you all to meet my grandmother who I hope is here with us in spirit. Most of you know that I think the only real death is being forgotten, and as long as we remember someone, they are alive with us. So, Laura, if you aren't playing cards or dancing, I hope you'll join us." I paused a moment and then continued.

"My grandmother had quite a few ideas about life and death and God and heaven, and she never hesitated to share them with all who'd listen. She had cancer, and lived with it for many years before she died. They didn't have all the terrific medicines that they have today, so she mostly just willed herself to stay alive until she was ready to go. But she told me that when the invitation came, she'd be happy to accept."

"Not me," said Bessie, who is eighty-seven and suffering with bone cancer. "I'm not going out easy. I'll be kicking and screaming for one more day. I love life. I love being alive. I love looking at the day."

"Bessie, you ramble on. I've heard you say a hundred times that you can't wait to die and join your loved ones," I said.

"Well, sometimes that's true, but on a day like this I want to live forever."

"Me too," said Robert, who is sixteen and has AIDS. "But I won't live forever and so I enjoy every day I have. I have a rule. I don't make plans. I don't dream or pretend what I'll be when I grow up. I do one day at a time. That way I never feel cheated."

"I want to grow up and be a ballerina and fly to Europe on the Concorde and meet Princess Di. I want to grow old someday and be a grandmother. But I'll probably never do any of those things," said Lisa, seven.

"Well, honey, I'm seventy-five and I never did any of those things either, but I did a lot more than I thought I would."

"Me too," replied Peter, who is ten. "Before I got sick I never did anything. Now I do all kinds of stuff between my chemo. My dad says I have a big menu, and a full plate. I guess that means I want to take a bite out of everything. Do you all know about Auntie Mame? Mister Silly told us about her. She's this really neat lady who takes care of her nephew, and teaches him all kinds of great stuff. She says that life is a banquet and most people are starving to death. Well, I'm not. I'm tasting every-thing. I may not get to be old, but I want to experience as much as I can before I die."

"You're as wise as Abraham," remarked Seth, who is in his sixties and has "buried two wives and three children."

"Does being old hurt?" asked Lisa who is seven.

"It hurts your pride and breaks your back," replied Seth.

"Huh?"

"Well, darling, I mean that life bends you over and makes your back ache, and it hurts your feelings—your pride—that you can't do the same things you could when you were younger."

"But, you can do more things when you're older," said Lisa.

"So?"

"Like go to the movies without an adult."

"Very true, darling, but when you get old you can't go to the movies without a nurse."

Everyone laughed.

The picnics became a regular thing that we all looked forward to. Like all the groups in the world of the dying, one member accepted the invitation and died. It was Peter.

As we sat together remembering him—honoring him—I recalled that first day we had all enjoyed our first picnic together. I recalled his big menu-big plate attitude and I suggested that we dedicate this day to him.

"Fine," replied Seth, "so let him pick up the check."

T I M E

I suppose we have all been subjected to the expression, "Don't put off until tomorrow what you can do today." And if you like a sunny day as much as I do, you know that a snooze in the hammock is much more fun than mowing the lawn and cleaning the garage.

When we enter the phase of "bargaining," we are stalling for time. We are delaying the inevitable—and we are missing the point. One reason I put so much emphasis on closing with the one you love is that it puts an end to bargaining and stalling. By facing the truth about an approaching death we can get on with the business of life, and living it.

Kids seem to understand this instinctively. They say, "Oh, I'm going to die. Let's go outside and toss the ball." They hardly miss a beat of life. To them it is almost a momentary glitch in the process—a hiccup—then it's back to the ball game.

My friend Kelly loves softball, and she loves winning. When we first met, she had just completed another series of chemo and was headed out to play ball. Her parents were as wrung out as a dishrag, but she was perky as a spring robin—Time's a wastin'!— Batter up!

The doctors told her parents she didn't have long to live. That was years ago. They were wrong. Kelly showed them *how* to live. She doesn't go to support groups. She prefers her ball club—they support her better. Kelly has discovered that staying alive is based on *being* alive.

Like Kelly, Samantha—Sam, as she prefers to be called—loves sports. But cancer took her legs. So now she's a sports writer, and her stuff is published in adult newspapers. They don't know she's thirteen and sits in a wheelchair in front of her computer terminal. They just know one thing: she's good.

Each of us has our own personal hourglass measuring out our days, one grain of sand at a time. But no one can see how full the glass is, or how empty.

One of the worst questions a person facing death asks is, "How much time do I have left?" The truth is, no one knows for sure, and I suspect that a lot of it has to do with attitude, inner perspective, and guts.

When AIDS first appeared in America it had already killed thousands around the world. At the present moment, it is always fatal. Not one has been cured, completely. But what we are learning now is that PWAs can live a long time. Studies of long-time survivors indicate that mental and emotional attitudes play a major role in prolonging life. Doesn't surprise me at all, the mind is a powerful healer.

The real answer to the question "How much time do I have left?" is in the unspoken part of the question itself. If you see the hourglass as half empty you are asking "How much time do I have left before I die?"

But if you see your hourglass the way children see theirs—still half full—the question becomes "How much time do I have left to live my life to the fullest?"

It's easy to see which question is better.

B O B B Y

Bobby had been in and out of remission for more than three years. His family, like all the families of terminal children, lived on an emotional roller coaster—in a limbo of not knowing, the real and awful Twilight Zone of terminal illness.

Finally, it became clear that Bobby would die soon, and his parents began to prepare themselves for the inevitable. They were not heroic, but they were strong. They were not particularly religious, but they knew there was a God and they trusted Him. They searched for and found inner strength and some degree of understanding for what was happening to them and to their child. They were in their early thirties. Bobby was eight.

We had been working together for three years, and as the time came for them to prepare for Bobby's death they wanted to arrange a last wish closing for him. Maybe they could get one of the organizations like Rainbow or Make a Wish to send them to Disneyland. I suggested we talk it over with Bobby.

"Bobby, how'd you like to go to Disneyland?" asked his dad.

"I want to ride with the Hell's Angels," replied Bobby.

His parents recoiled in horror. His father had practically been born in a three-piece suit, and his mother would put Donna Reed to shame.

"The Hell's Angels!" they gasped. "Wouldn't you rather meet Mickey Mouse?"

"No. I want to ride with the Angels and I want a black leather motorcycle jacket and I want a tattoo and an earring too!"

"Arggggh!" they moaned.

"We could go to Sea World?"

"No, it's my wish, and I want to ride with the Hell's Angels."

"Maybe we could get Mickey to wear a leather jacket," they pleaded desperately.

"Look," I said. "If I can arrange this, will you let him do it?"

They looked at me and said, "Are you crazy?"

"I used to ride with a motorcycle club when I was younger and they can be very nice guys."

"Their women are tattooed!" cried Bobby's mother.

"Let's go outside and talk this over."

We sat in the hospital coffee shop and I quietly explained my idea to them.

"I know some weekend warriors. They're really very nice guys, businessmen, doctors, lawyers; they ride motorcycles. Their women aren't tattooed. Maybe I can arrange something. How about it?"

They held each other's hands, and I knew that they were in a lot of pain. I knew they would give Bobby anything they could, but I also knew they wanted this closing to be something they could think back on after Bobby died. We had spoken so often about this final memory, and the good it would do for all of them. I knew that an outing with a motorcycle gang was the last thing they had imagined.

They finally agreed. I went to a local cycle club and explained the situation. Told them how this little boy wanted to ride with the Angels and have a leather jacket and a tattoo. And they said, "You got it, man. We'll fix it up."

So two weekends later, on a bright and sunny Sunday morning, they arrived: thirty-five of them—on motorcycles, wearing their black leather motorcycle jackets. The lead bike had a sidecar for Bobby to ride in, and when his parents brought him downstairs, the bikers presented him with his own motorcycle jacket with the club patch sewn on back.

They gently put him in the sidecar, and we took off for Bear Mountain. This is a favorite run of local bikers, and the trip along the Palisades Parkway is one of the most beautiful in the area.

What I didn't know was that they had arranged for three more clubs to join us on the other side of the George Washington Bridge. There they were, lined up along the highway, cheering Bobby as he sped past. The roar of engines was deafening as they joined up behind us, and we arrived, one hundred and fifty strong, at the Bear Mountain picnic site that they had prearranged. We spent the whole day doing motorcycle events, games and tricks and races.

And Bobby was part of it all. His parents watched and were amazed by the love and tenderness—the sheer kindness of these bikers. They watched the whirlwind of events, and all their preconceived notions reconceived. And, by day's end, they were different people.

Bobby was the center of attention every minute of the day. He got a rub-on tattoo. He got an earring. And he got the greatest gift of all, his wish come true.

But that's not the best part of this story. That's the part about the kindness of strangers and wishes granted and closure and making a memory and having heart.

When Billy died, he was buried in his black leather motorcycle jacket. His parents invited the bike clubs to be the honor guard for his funeral cortege, and they accepted.

In my mind, no Viking king had a better procession on his journey to Valhalla, and I felt privileged to have had a hand in it.

It made my heartache easier to bear.

WISDOM

A wise man once said that wisdom was not knowing *what* the answers are but knowing *where* the answers are.

In my case, the answers have come from all the children who have touched my life during the past few years. From them I learned the real meaning of truth and fearlessness and love.

In return for these gifts, I have given them laughter, my undivided attention, and my unconditional love.

They have made me wiser than any *fool* should be, and have enriched my life beyond my wildest dreams.

And they have given me the answer to the question, "Where is heaven?"

It is in your heart.

E P I L O G U E

ROBERT DIED AS THE leaves turned gold and started to fall. Those who knew Robert from Harmony and who were able went up to Harlem with me for the funeral. I hadn't been to Harlem since the late 1950s, when I used to hit the jazz clubs and line up at the Apollo to hear the greats do their thing. I wondered if Robert's funeral would be in the great Baptist tradition of joyous singing, and I asked Mary if she knew the family. Yes, she replied, they were definitely old-time Baptists, and there would be a lot of singing.

We all piled into the limo I had hired and headed uptown. The Eggheads had decided to go bald as a tribute to Robert, whose honesty and strut were an inspiration to us all. We wore the folded red ribbons that honor those who die of AIDS.

"Does Robert's family know we're coming?" asked Timmy.

"Yes," replied Mary. "They know, darlin', and they are very pleased. We are invited to the house after the service. Gonna be lots of wonderful soul food for you white kids to pig out on."

"Why is it called soul food, Mary?"

"Because it is cooked with heart, and enriches your spirit as well as your belly, and because colored folks got the copyright on that word and use it everywhere. Why we even got soul jeans just like the Jewish folks got the Levis."

"Mary, you're going to warp these children's minds with your funnin'," I teased.

"Got to keep them on their toes," she replied with a broad smile.

We sat together towards the rear of the church. Mary sat near the aisle, and after the minister had finished speaking, he asked her to come forward and sing with the choir. She eased herself out of the pew, smoothed her dress and strode up to the choir. The piano player struck a few notes, and suddenly Mary's powerful voice filled the church. In that moment I knew in my heart that she could have had a professional career, could probably have sung opera at the Met. Instead she had chosen to care for dying children. Now she sang for one of them. Sang about God and heaven and joy. Sang about love with love, sang about pain with pain, sang about loss with all the loss she felt.

When she finished, Robert's mother hugged her. There they stood, two big black woman holding one another and crying for the baby that was gone.

We went to the party afterwards, and did indeed eat soul food—but the soul food that nourished me most was the sound of Mary singing. I wasn't the only one who felt that way, because I overheard Timmy ask Mary something that filled my heart to the brim.

He asked her if she would sing for him when he died.

Mary just smiled.

There is a great deal of truth to the expression, "help is just a phone call away." Today, thankfully, there are a number of local and national hot lines that provide help and counseling twenty-four hours a day. There are also hundreds of support groups for almost every need.

For parents and family members who are either facing the possibility of a child's death or grieving the death of a child, there is a wonderful national organization called The Compassionate Friends, which is made up of parents who have lost a child to death. They also have a national newsletter.

For information, write to:

The Compassionate Friends
    Newsletter
P.O. Box 3696
Oak Brook, Illinois 60522–3696

Libraries and bookstores generally have sections devoted to subjects concerning illness, death, and grieving. However, these may be limited in scope. There are three mail-order companies that specialize in books on these subjects as well as in a variety of books specifically for children.

These catalogs are all free and available to individuals and organizations:

The Rainbow Collection
477 Hannah Branch Road
Burnsville, North Carolina 28714
Phone: (704) 675–5909

Compassion Book Service
479 Hannah Branch Road
Burnsville, North Carolina 28714
Phone: (704) 675–9670

Centering Corporation
1531 North Saddle Creek Road
Omaha, Nebraska 68104
Phone: (402) 553–1200

If you would like to ask a question or share an experience, you are welcome to write to me personally, c/o:

The Harmony Project
Box 28K
300 East 40th Street
New York, NY 10016